The Assault On Freedom In America

Mac Taylor

The Assault On Freedom In America

ISBN: 978-1-945975-75-2

Published by EA Books Publishing a division of
Living Parables of Central Florida, Inc. a 501c3
EABooksPublishing.com

DEDICATION

This book is dedicated to my daughter Ana Taylor, and our Revolutionary War ancestors as well as all the other colonial American patriots who fought and died for the great cause of human freedom. Freedom which they gifted to all Americans by their sacrifices.

Nathan Bond
Roger Brown
Turner Christian
Issac David
Zachariah Dickerson
Private Eli Eavenson
Larkin Gatewood
Captain Aaron Higginbotham
Captain John Higginbotham
Colonel Samuel Higginbotham
Thomas Hilley
James Hunt
John Jordan
*Reverend Thomas Maxwell
William Nelms
John Norman
Captain Robert Pulliam
Ann Satterwhite
Samuel Shepherd
David Staples
Jeremiah Terrell
Dozier Thornton
Mark Thornton
John Upshaw
James Vaughan

* Reverend Thomas Maxwell, my 6th great grandfather, was a Baptist preacher and a Revolutionary War soldier. He was born on September 8, 1742, in Middlesex County, Virginia. He died on December 12, 1837, in Hart County Georgia. In 1788 he founded Falling Creek Baptist Church near Elberton in Elbert County, Georgia. He later preached for 30 years at Holly Springs Baptist (a church he also helped found) in Elbert County Georgia until the year 1826. In Virginia, before the revolution started he was jailed

multiple times by the British Authorities for preaching the Baptist faith, a gospel that didn't agree with the official doctrine of the Anglican church, the Official Church of England in the Virginia Colony. On one occasion, it is said, Reverend Thomas Maxwell was hauled right out of the pulpit by British authorities while preaching. He continued to preach in jail and he converted the jailer and his entire family to Christianity. He later served in the Culpepper Militia in Virginia during the American Revolution. His defense lawyer when he was jailed for preaching was his nearby neighbor—Patrick Henry.

> "Posterity! You will never know how much it cost the present generation to preserve your freedom. I hope you will make good use of it. If you do not, I shall repent in heaven that I ever took half the pains to preserve it."
>
> John Adams, April 26, 1777

ACKNOWLEDGEMENTS

No Man is an Island
John Donne, 1624

No man is an island entire of itself;
every man is a piece of the continent,
a part of the main.
If a clod be washed away by the sea,
Europe is the less,
as well as if a promontory were,
as well as if a manor of thy friend's
or thine own were.
Any man's death diminishes me,
because I am involved in mankind;
and therefore never send to know
for whom the bell tolls;
it tolls for thee.

I am not an island unto myself thus I want to give my heartfelt thanks to the following who participated in this work and are therefore most assuredly a part of this project. I thank God from whom all blessings come and for the ability to complete this work. A posthumous debt of gratitude and thanks to my mom and dear friend Helen Skelton Taylor and my dad Clinton Franklin Taylor who gave me the benefit of their wisdom, love, and knowledge of life. My daughter Ana, the inspiration for this book because I want your future to be lived in freedom. Ana, thank you for your enthusiastic support throughout this project.

To my life-long friend John Hayes MD, thank you for the tireless work ethic you gave to my book, for your piercing insight, straight forward honesty, and to-the-point critical reviews. To Jason Arledge "Jake" and Rebecca Arledge for giving me a break from writing and taking me out to the Gulf Stream on the m/v Pura Vida to fish and clear the cobwebs. I also thank all my other crew-friends of the m/v Pura Vida for their friendship and support. Jake thank you for always pointing to true on life's compass in the fog of things, my writing, and other stuff. I'm honored to call you friend. To Edward Taylor for always being there throughout this project. For reading my work when it counted and the great and timely reviews and feedback. Your encouragement has meant tons, thank you Eddie. To Roberto Gonzalez Anaya I thank you for your reading and critical reviews. I could always count on you for offering your honest and independent viewpoints and that meant a lot to this project, thank you. To Sam Markham Tedder, thank you for your consistent and encouraging support. To Jonathon Dunne, an Irishman and Dubliner who is as American at heart than any American I know, thank you for the great job writing the foreword. To Teresa Dickerson Bruton, thank you for your tremendous contribution to this project through your exhaustive genealogy research of our family. The ancestry details that you have contributed have made a wonderful addition to this book. To Linda Gilden my editor. Thank you for of your tireless dedication to this book. It is a much better book because of your participation. I appreciate your hard work, honest opinions, professional guidance, and insights, etc., thank you very much. To my publisher Cheri Cowell and team at EA Books Publishing, I thank all of you for the professional quality and care that you exhibited towards the production of this book.

TABLE OF CONTENTS

FOREWORD

STOP! Look around for a minute and take a mental note of what life is like for you right now. Our world is changing so rapidly that your life could be incredibly different next week, next year or five years from now. Tomorrow brings the potential for exciting changes—it could be a new currency based on blockchain, a self-driving car, robots and artificial intelligence, people living on Mars or simple things like how we are changing our purchasing habits from retail to online vendors.

Our culture in society is also changing. Tyranny is on the march, and presents itself in many forms – we have countless oppressive dictators, theocracy, and terrorist groups who offer a hard tyranny that kills any individual who does not fall in line. We are also witnessing a softer, more "compassionate" kind of tyranny that has become socially acceptable in the western world, represented under the label of democracy and from democratically elected politicians who serve in parliaments.

Today, not only have different versions of socialism gained mainstream credibility, but an increasing number of people are accepting government control in EVERY aspect of their lives, once their side has the power, in exchange for some phony notion of security, or the belief that politicians somehow know better than you. If you consider that to be an outrageous statement, I would ask you to identify the part of your life in which there is no government involvement.

Government controls how your house is built, and where it can be built. Every product you purchase and use MUST be approved by the government – everything from the car you drive, to a sandwich at the local deli, to the toilet you use. It controls the terms of your employment, has access to your calls and emails, decides how much of your hard-earned money you can keep, and now controls the narrative of what speech is deemed politically correct. And this is why we are also witnessing society's extreme elements rise up again, claiming to be the champion for the people they represent and we see this on many sides. So, how did we get here? More importantly, what can you do to get involved?

"History Does Not Repeat Itself, But It Rhymes."

This famous quote often attributed to Mark Twain perfectly describes the history of our world. The history of our world can be summed up in three words – TYRANNY, CONTROL, and HATE!

The sad truth is that the vast majority of people who have ever lived have experienced some version of tyranny - all that changes is the times in which they live, the people who control them, how they exercised control, and who they blamed for the failures in society.

We can go all the way back to the Pharaohs and how they treated the ancient Egyptians, to famous dynasties, to kings and queens, to great empires that never had the sun set on them, up to the modern North Korean dictator, Russian oligarchs, and Iranian theocrats.

We can also add countless contemporary ideologies, including variations of Marxism, Communism, Socialism, Progressivism, Nazism, Fascism, Populism, Tribalism, Nationalism, and the wolf in sheep's clothing—Democracy.

Every one of these ideologies is rooted in tyranny and seeks to control the individual, for either personal gain or for some perceived notion of the "common good." These rulers and ideologies all share similar core ideals. So, what are they?

Tyranny Core Beliefs

- Life is disposable and nothing more than a resource.
- Rights always come from the "powerful."
- Belief in the collective.
- All men shall be judged by a set of labels and / or by their background.
- You can only follow the passions the "powerful" deem appropriate.
- You can only enjoy the fruits of your labor that the "powerful" do not want for themselves.
- You need the "powerful" to change the world: you cannot do it!
- Power always starts at the top, and works its way down.
- There are no limits on government.
- Man is the ultimate authority.

In life, there is usually an exception to the rule and norm. In the history of the world, there is one exception to the norm of tyranny: That exception is the idea of America. This idea was, and still is, the exact opposite to what the world preaches, and it changed the world so much that we are still reaping the benefits over 240 years later. This idea has certain key principles:

Freedom's Core Beliefs

- Life is precious, and a right.
- Rights come from your Creator.
- All men are created equal.
- You are free to pursue your happiness.
- You can keep and enjoy the fruits of your labor.
- Culture is focused around the individual and the family.
- You don't need anyone to change the world – *you* can do it!
- The role of government is to secure and protect rights for all.
- Power is with the individual.
- Ultimate authority is GOD and nature.

Tear Down Society

The differences between tyranny and freedom run deep into the cultures of society. The culture of tyranny promotes jealousy of others' success and possessions. This is done by demeaning people, creating the illusion of being powerless, that there is some boogey man holding them down, and they will never be able to make positive changes in their lives. The end result of this society is people seeking to tear down others, and enjoying their downfall because if I can't have something, why should someone else have it. That's not fair!

America was the exact opposite – through the ideals of freedom, America encouraged people to strive for a version of the "American Dream" – a dream where you control your destiny and you can make something of your life. Your society celebrated those rags-to-riches stories because it provided society with motivation and the belief that said, "Hey if they can do it, why can't I? After all they have nothing I don't have access to."

Brotherhood

One of the crucial ways the "powerful" keep their position is to create proxy wars within society. These proxy wars take many different forms, but the aim is always the same – to ensure the people are divided and HATE other parts of society. It manifests itself in battles that you witness every day around the world as the powerful divide us into groups like: rich vs. poor, white vs. color, male vs. female, gay vs. straight, left vs. right. For power and control they simply pit group against group against group, etc.

If these proxy wars are successful, the end result is always the same - ALL sides of the argument are looking at the other, seeing an enemy who needs to be defeated and crushed.

Once again, America was built on an idea that is the exact opposite - "E Pluribus Unum," which means "out of many, one." America's founding fathers understood that you will always have deep differences in beliefs and ideologies, but at the end of the debate, both sides are still Americans and are part of the solution.

This point was so critical to America's success that when President George Washington wrote his farewell address to the nation, he made it his first warning. He wrote,

> The unity of government which constitutes you ONE people is also now dear to you. It is justly so, for it is a main pillar in the edifice of your real independence, the support of your tranquility at home, your peace abroad; of your safety; of your prosperity; of that very liberty

> which you so highly prize. But as it is easy to foresee that, from different causes and from different quarters, much pains will be taken, many artifices employed to weaken in your minds the conviction of this truth; as this is the point in your political fortress against which the batteries of internal and external enemies will be most constantly and actively (though often covertly and insidiously) directed, it is of infinite moment that you should properly estimate the immense value of your national union to your collective and individual happiness that you should cherish a cordial, habitual, and immovable attachment to it; accustoming yourselves to think and speak of it as of the palladium of your political safety and prosperity; watching for its preservation with jealous anxiety; discountenancing whatever may suggest even a suspicion that it can in any event be abandoned; and indignantly frowning upon the first dawning of every attempt to alienate any portion of our country from the rest, or to enfeeble the sacred ties which now link together the various parts.

So how can you make a difference?

Today you see many different efforts in America claiming to be the solution to the problem. They range from the Article Five movement, to term limits, to supporting your current President. While they may all have noble intentions, and I believe movements like Article Five have the potential to make a huge difference, they all pale in comparison to the number one solution – educate yourself, and then share your education with others on the principles of both freedom and tyranny.

Let me be crystal clear – I DO NOT mean simply converting others to vote the way you do. I mean by doing research on the labels I mentioned above, by reading this book and many others to increase your awareness, knowledge, and understanding of America and our world, and why the ideals of Freedom are the only ones that are eternally true and the only ones to have ever led to success.

In Closing

As an Irishman and an outsider, I don't believe in any President, Congress, or Supreme Court to save America or make it great. I share the sentiments of the great Alexis de Tocqueville when he spoke about America being great because Americans are good. I believe and have faith in each and every one of you. It is your everyday actions (regardless of how you vote) and working together, that will reaffirm America's destiny of goodness and goodwill.

Every American is special and will play a key role in the survival and the future prosperity of America.

I look forward to joining you at every opportunity as we learn from our past and our shared human experience. We can be part of a generation that paints a picture of the future where everyone is free to control their own lives, and of what America can be, what it should be, and what it will become – A Beacon of HOPE for the rest of the world, and a great encouragement to the world to follow the principles of *real* freedom! Together we can stand against *The Assault On Freedom In America*.

Jonathon Dunne
Freedomsdisciple.com

EXPLANATION OF IMPORTANT TERMS

Natural Law:

Natural law is the inherent and universal principles found in nature. Natural law is the basis for man's general interpretation of what is right and what is wrong. The natural laws are discoverable to man through man's reasoning abilities. Some examples of laws derived from natural law are our laws confirming: that theft is wrong, a natural right to property ownership, that murder is wrong, the natural right to free speech, and the natural right to personal privacy. These are but a few examples that man has *reasoned* from universal natural law—law which exists in nature itself. We have implemented the principles of natural law into our constitutional government in order to create a just structure for our civil society. Natural law is foundational to any just civil order. Other examples of natural law are the universal laws of mathematics, physics, biology, etc. The laws of science are found in nature, just as the basic natural laws of moral behavior, and exist independent of man's control. They form the basis for man's scientific discovery and inventions.

Conservative:

The word conservative has many contexts for its use. For example, if we are talking about spending habits, a person could be a conservative or liberal spender. Someone else may be considered to be morally liberal and another morally conservative. One person may want a liberal amount of ice cream while another may prefer a more conservative amount. This word conservative is one of the most misused and misunderstood terms in our society today. In my experience, far too many people confuse or fuse this term with their lifestyle choices, moral viewpoint, or when they are speaking of their view of the proper role of government. So if we are talking about government and you have a classical liberal "live and let live" philosophy, you believe in the individual right of a person to choose his lifestyle, religion, sexual preferences; you believe in free markets; the right to keep the money you have earned; the right of free speech. If you believe in the right of the individual to be left alone to pursue his happiness free from excessive government interference, etc., then you are a conservative regarding your view of the role of government regardless of your life choices. You may be liberal or conservative in your personal lifestyle or the amount of ice cream you eat, but in that context, the word has absolutely nothing to do with your view of government. A conservative government is one that is limited in its size and scope. A conservative government supports freedom of the individual where people are governed by *consent*, not mandates or other forces. The American Constitution is a conservative document, not because of the religious and or moral beliefs of the founders, but because it describes a design of a limited and minimal federal government and thus, when abided by, maximal liberty is enjoyed by its citizens.

Liberal:

The word liberal, like the word conservative, also has many contextual uses. For example, if we define a lifestyle, spending habit, or even the amount of ice cream one prefers, the word liberal conveys certain ideas. Ideas like liberal or free lifestyle, liberal or free spending, and lots or a liberal amount of ice cream. However, if we talk about the role of government, the word liberal has quite a different meaning. A liberal government, in current parlance, means an expanding growing government with ever increasing regulations and power over our lives. A liberal government which regulates the many aspects of our society, economy, and even our behavior. Therefore, if we are defining the role of government and you believe that the federal government should be used to implement a forced societal structure which imposes the beliefs of some onto the larger society by the force of law; if you believe the state is the grantor of rights and you do not believe in the natural rights of the individual; if you believe a one-size politically correct lifestyle fits all and the government should be used to force this view and outcome on the people; the government has a right to take money you earn and give to another person via taxation through redistribution; that it is a proper role of the government to impose fairness and equality of outcome of the citizenry; then you are most assuredly a liberal in your idea of the role of government. A government that is expansive and has a long regulatory reach over the particulars of our individual lives. A government that controls us rather than protects our individual rights and defends our individual freedom. If the previous describes you, then you are more fitting to the next category of liberals, see below. However, if you are a liberal person in your lifestyle and beliefs but you believe in a limited government that respects the God-given rights of individuals to live according to their conscience—you may want to sit down for this—then you are a conservative in your view of the proper role of government.

Statists:

The progressive, socialist, authoritarian, Marxist, totalitarian, communist, and dictator are all *statists*. Statists use government to control and regulate our lives to suit their worldview. How they think society, culture, and an economy should be planned and managed—by them. Statists do this through their creation of seemingly endless laws, regulations, and other government forces. Each of the above political ideologies is from the same family tree of those seeking government control over the individual.

In stark contrast to statists, our American constitutional system is one of individual liberty, individual rights, and government by consent of the governed only. Individual liberty is paramount in the U.S. Constitution, and the citizens are not to be lorded over by the state. These Statists' ideologies, however, are like incestuous cousins to one another and the only difference between them is the methods they employ. Think of it this way: imagine we are in a room filled with ten or twenty people. We are all human, but we are not all the same. We each have our unique differences and preferences.

The same is true of statists. If, for example, you have a room full of socialists, post modern liberals, progressives, Marxists, communists, dictators, etc., they are all statists and believe in the power of the state over the individual. The difference is that each has their unique differences and preferences to enforce government power over the individual. A difference of methodology, not ideology. The dictator or communist will exercise harsh rule from the outset, while the progressive or statist may seem to be less harsh at the outset. The communist state controls all property and prohibits private ownership of property. The Socialist State allows private ownership of property, but it controls your property through burdensome and seemingly endless regulations, fees, and taxes. The communist state controls the means of production by owning it, while the socialist state controls the means of production through regulation but lets you own it and pay the taxes. The more rules, regulations, restrictions, and taxes, the more the state has control over you, your property, and your life. The point is they all eventually end up in the same rotten tree of government force over individual rights and freedom. The lines between the various statists' ideologies overlap because they have many areas of agreement and commonality. Because of the inherent areas of commonality, no single individual definitions precisely describe each of the terms. This is also why you often hear the terms used in a combined fashion. For example: communists dictator, progressive socialist, Democratic Socialist Party of America (DSA), Marxist socialism, social progressives, etc. To get caught up in definitions and become confused by the often hair-splitting differences between the statists is to miss the point. The point to understand is that the statist, with his many masks, stands at odds with our American constitutional system of liberty and individual rights.

Political Correctness:

Political correctness, or PC for short, has its roots in statist authoritarian rule. In the 20th century, the term was used to describe the communist and socialist requirement that their members adhere to the party line in their speech and conduct. Hence the phrase to "tow the commie line." The very notion of political correctness is antithetical or in opposition to freedom and America. Political correctness attempts to piggy back upon the natural moral law with its emotionally appealing lure of not offending anyone.

Political correctness is an emotionally based tactic not grounded in reason. What used to be basic common moral sense has been, in far too many circles, replaced by the PC party line or more specifically PC speech codes. To be sure, both common moral sense and PC can affect the way people speak to one another. But one of these is a moral code imposter. PC is a concoction of arbitrary man-made speech codes masquerading as a way of expressing respect and kindness to one another. It is anything but. A better description would be speech bondage married to confusion and chaos. PC divides and separates people; it does not bring them together. PC carries with it the burden and restraints of an ever increasing and harshly enforced speech code. The natural moral law is innate to each human, therefore, it peaceably promotes harmony, unity, and calm, as it appeals to the individual heart of each of us. The teaching of natural moral law encourages us as individuals in society to self-regulate and offer mutual love and respect to one another. With natural moral law, we self-impose and enforce the universal and eternal moral virtues upon ourselves as individuals, and this supports our freedom. Virtues like patience, kindness, respect for others and their property, loving your neighbor as yourself, etc. This is in large part what our Founders meant by self-rule. Morality is a prerequisite to freedom. In contrast, Political Correctness demands adherence to the ever-changing and expanding speech codes. Speech codes must be imposed upon the individual and or group by an outside regulatory force. This steps on the toes of freedom. As PC

Marxism progresses, it will be a very bitter pill to swallow if we do not stop it now. Which road shall we take America?

Social Justice:

Social Justice is a manipulated modification of the concept of justice. This modification by adding the word social to the concept of justice changes the definition and the meaning of the word justice. Justice, when properly applied, is an individual concept. Social justice is a group concept. Let me give you an example. Suppose you are a member of a certain racial group and that group decides to steal numerous items from the local supermarket. The crime is committed by the group, but you did not take part in the crime. Nevertheless, you get arrested because you are part of that group per your racial makeup. You get sent to jail along with all the others in the group. Did you get justice? No, you did not, and more accurately you have been treated unjustly. An individual should not be judged by the group he or she may belong to. Human beings are individuals and should be respected and treated as such. Each according to his or her character and merit. Social Justice seeks to deny the individual and segment society into separate groups. Then the social justice advocates pit one group against the other in cunning ways.

They label the groups as the offenders and the offended, the aggressors and the aggrieved, the have and the have-nots, the rich and the poor, the privileged and the unprivileged, the right and the left, the black and the white, majority and minority, etc. After each group has been labeled the group seen as the disadvantaged group is encouraged to demand *social justice* from the group seen as being advantaged. Social Justice then seeks to take from the one group and hand what has been taken to the other group. If it is money being taken from the wealthy, they call it economic justice. If it is racial quotas being sought after, they call it racial justice. Social Justice is simply the Marxist socialist tactic of equality of outcome which creates division and strife. Social Justice is false benevolence with an emotional lure of good feeling and fairness. It is deception seeking to hide under the word justice in order stealthily perform its Marxist dirty work. America is not about social or favored-group justice. American is about equal justice under the law.

Cultural Marxism:

Cultural Marxism is a planned assault on freedom and western culture by Marxists. Cultural Marxism is the implementation of the tactics of political correctness, social justice, and multiculturalism to destroy western culture, capitalism, and therefore freedom. This is the same Marxist wolf wrapped in a new sheepskin called cultural Marxism. Marxists initially sought to create a revolution in the West by encouraging the labor classes to overthrow the upper classes in the early 20th century. The class warfare tactic did not work, however, because freedom and capitalism provided the working people with a nice life. Thus, they were not interested in a Marxist revolution. The first attempt to assault the west failed, so the long march through western culture was hypothesized and initiated as yet another attempt to destroy western freedom. The long march through the west is designed to infiltrate and corrupt all western culture and institutions etc. It is a simple divide and conquer strategy. It is called the long march because it takes decades to implement. Why? Because first you have to infiltrate the cultural institutions in order to destroy them from the inside out, and this takes time. This is what we are witnessing in America today. The destruction of our culture on many fronts through political correctness, social justice, and multiculturalism. The long march has been going on for about 100 years. However, it has now grown and intensified to a level that the average person can see the cultural destruction, division, and animosity between groups and individuals taking place. Cultural Marxism is working just as hypothesized and we must recognize this for what it is, in order to stop it. Far too many of our institutions have been infiltrated, and thus we have a lot of work to do. Sadly, Cultural Marxism is now deeply rooted in our country, and we freedom loving Americans are just beginning to wake up to this reality. The time to stand is upon us.

INTRODUCTION

A Prophetic Warning from our First President - George Washington

It's early fall, and the evening is one of those cool, clear and crisp evenings that you so enjoy. The leaves are beginning to turn and there seems a new rhythm in the air. An upbeat happy one. A most welcome change from the heat of a long hot urban summer. You are in the Big Apple, yes, good ol' New York, New York. After having a wonderful dinner with friends you are attending a much anticipated play on Broadway.

You and your friends are watching a political play. A play not unlike those of Shakespeare. This one, however, is a contemporary political satire. The subject matter is of the current goings on in the country. Many moments of high drama and intense emotions. Serious undertones with implications of real life consequence and, fortunately, there is comedic relief. It is a play after all. The play is nicely balanced between the serious and the comedic. It leans to the comedic side and the audience seems fully engaged and having a very good experience.

At some point deep into Act II, several audience members, so caught up in the drama on stage clamor over and through the orchestra pit and onto the stage themselves. The audience gasps at first, then seems to hold its collective breath not knowing if this is part of the production or not. The would be actors run the gamut from young to old. They begin to yell and shout, while taking up political sides as if they are part of the play. The audience, still uncertain of what is happening is brimming with anticipation to find out. Soon, as security officers begin to arrest and remove the interlopers, it becomes all too obvious these would be participants are not part of the play at all. The audience, still in shock over the whole episode, awaits its cue from the actors themselves.

The actors are clearly disheveled and upset. An hour-long intermission is necessary before the play can continue.

Suppose this actually happened to you as an audience member or an actor. What would you think of such persons? I have a few choice words in my mind. See if you agree. Inconsiderate, ignorant, selfish, uninformed, riotous, emotional, and irrational. You may have a few others of your own, but my guess is that we are most likely in general agreement.

Shakespeare, in *As You Like It* - Act II Scene VII, wrote these words for his character Jaques, “All the world’s a stage, and all the men and women merely players; they have their exits and their entrances...”

What a great line and so true. All the world is a stage and we are all actors upon it. Unlike Broadway, however, the world stage is real and has real world consequences. Consequences that follow the decisions and actions we take. Our actions can have the consequence of causing human pain, suffering, death, and any manner or sort of human misery imaginable. Our actions can have the opposite outcome as well. A positive outcome that uplifts, helps, gives comfort to, etc. others. This is true as individuals, and it is true as a culture and country. Therefore, would it not be wise to consider our actions as best we can - before taking them? And in order to consider our actions, is it not important or, in fact, absolutely necessary for the responsible actor to be properly informed prior to taking any action? To do less, we risk doing unknown harm to someone even though we may have the best of all intentions. It is one thing to have an opinion. It is quite another to know "why" you hold a certain opinion. One you can explain and support by reason and sound principle without yelling or causing harm to another. If you struggle with that perhaps you are not as informed as you ought to be. We are all guilty of not being as informed as we ought to be at some time and in some aspect or another in our lives. But we should strive to become as informed as possible before we take actions that may impact another person's life - for good or ill.

Each of us must recognize that the play of humanity has been going on for thousands of years prior to any one of us taking our first breath in this world. The real life drama of man has a deep and long history. For anyone of us to pretend that we can just jump on stage and start playing a role is as foolhardy as those imaginary actors jumping on the stage of Broadway. When we take such ill-informed actions we risk real life harm to others, quite possibly ourselves, and to our posterity. Our collective ignorance may well cost us our freedom if we continue down our country's current path.

Do you know what the notorious communist Vladimir Lenin called such people? He called them "useful idiots." The useful idiot, as spoken of by Lenin, is generally naive, uninformed, and guided more by emotion rather than passion bridled by calm reason. Therefore, easily used and manipulated to the benefit of the mischievous power hungry politician and the detriment of our individual sovereign freedom. An emotionalized mob can be a powerful force for any would-be tyrant-minded, unprincipled politician to wield. Unprincipled power seekers have invariably taken the advantage of "useful idiots" throughout history in order to gain the reins of power. And once power is gained, history proves, they have and will use physical violent force in order to keep it, to the point of killing those who disagree. Ignorance risks empowering the dangerous unprincipled man. Being as informed as possible in the principles of human individual freedom and *why* America came to be, is our only hopeful antidote to this danger.

George Washington–our first President gave his famous Farewell Address to the people of the United States on September 17, 1796. Our first president, having led our young country through a revolution for the sovereign liberty of man in America, was fully aware of past kings, queens, dictators, and tyrants who would never release the reins of power from their grasps. Much less, after having won a bloody revolution, turn around and hand the power of government to the people. This American idea of government by consent of the people was a radical departure from the injustice of tyranny of the people being ruled by a king. A people now enjoying the liberty of "self rule" by their consent became exciting news the world over. Government by the consent of the people was born in America and only in America. The American Revolution, with its basis fully explained in the Declaration of Independence, gave birth to a governmental structure unlike any government structure the world had ever seen. Kings, queens, dictators, and tyrants were dethroned, at least here in America. The law became king in America, as Thomas Paine said. And no man is above the law.

George Washington served two terms as President—then stepped aside. But he didn't just step aside silently and then move on. He left us with his Farewell Address. His address contained a prophetic warning to our country. Individual freedom was radical and new. The tyrant kings were not. The history of the tyranny of man by government was fresh in the minds of our forefathers and first President.

Wise in experience and knowledge George Washington writes, no he warns us, freedom has enemies. Enemies who will devise assaults against our freedom by assaulting our Constitution, culture, and other means. He states: "One method of *assault* may be to affect the forms of the Constitution, alterations which will impair the energy of the system, and thus undermine what cannot be directly overthrown."

In another example of his prophetic warning Washington talks of party politics with its various combinations of groups and associations. He says – "they are likely, in the course of time and things, to become potent engines, by which cunning, ambitious, and unprincipled men will be enabled to subvert the power of the people, and to usurp for themselves the reins of government; destroying afterward the very engines which have lifted them to unjust dominion." He continues to say these same men will make creative emotional or cunning appeals to us in order to make assaults upon our constitution and therefore our individual freedom. Further he says; we must be wise in understanding that our constitution is based upon *principles*, and principles do not change. He states that "you resist with care the spirit of innovation upon its principles, however specious the pretext." In other words, the constitution is not a living breathing document that should change with every passing whim or current fanciful popular idea. Remember he said cunning, ambitious, and unprincipled men will make these attempts at manipulating their way to undermining our constitution to gain power for themselves. Continuing to speak about party politics and its various special interest groups, Washington further writes that "it agitates the community with ill-founded jealousies and false alarms - kindles animosity of one party against another, foments occasionally riot and insurrection."

It is remarkable how deadly insightful George Washington was as to the ways in which unscrupulous men will attempt to manipulate the power of government to suit their own desires. One look at the daily news and one can't help but be struck by the wisdom, profound and insightful accuracy George Washington had in warning us there would be many assaults upon our individual freedom. I highly recommend you read Washington's Farewell Address, the Declaration of Independence, and our Constitution. It is important to read and know our founding documents in order to thwart the many schemes used to undermine it. Schemes which are aimed squarely as an assault upon our individual American freedom. What stands between you and your ability to self-determine your life with its many options open to you and a would be king, queen, dictator, tyrant, or progressive ruling you? The United States Constitution.

The American Constitution is still here but it has been impaired or weakened greatly from what it was as designed by our Founders. Many creative, unprincipled decisions have been ascribed to the Constitution over the past 100 or so years, that do not exist in the document itself. What does that mean in real terms? It means we are less free and more ruled by government than our founders were. It means the cunning and unprincipled men Washington warned us about have been successful in their effort to "subvert the power of the people" as Washington said. To subvert the power of the people means to subvert your freedom. Our constitutional individual freedom has been and is under assault just as George Washington warned.

American government exists to protect our individual rights and freedoms. It is not happenstance that we speak of individual rights, because your rights belong to you as an individual. You may be part of a group, but you are not a group. You are you and I am me, and no more. Identity politics, or group rights, is one of those cunning assaults envisioned by our first President. The group rights movement is a subtle and yet nefarious assault on your individual rights. This movement places us in groups thereby pitting us against one another. We then begin to see each other not as individuals but as members of a group. The good or favored group or the bad, unfavored group. This assigns a subtle message of prior guilt toward a person or persons who may be guilty of nothing more than exercising their beliefs and being part a group by choice or birth. This is a beginning tactic of serious political divisions. It is a red flag, a warning sign. We do not punish people for what they believe or simply because they may be part of a group. We punish people for illegal actions that they commit. To begin to punish people for what they believe or because of a group they are part of would be to subvert and, if successful, revert or revoke the American Constitution. There may be bad persons in a favored group and there may very well be good persons in an unfavored group. Cunning false divisions are being presented to us and some people are acting on this by beginning to express hate toward people for their group identity or what they may believe. This is an example of an assault to "undermine what cannot be directly overthrown," to quote George Washington. In this case it's a cunning assault on individual rights. Can you see the shrewd nature of this and how it creates agitation of the citizenry, just as Washington warned? Moreover, can you see how this leads to a diminution of the *individual* or in other words *you.*

The federal government was given only 17 enumerated powers. Washington D.C. is exercising power well beyond its constitutionally prescribed 17 enumerated boundaries. Washington D.C. has begun choosing sides in matters of personal choice, belief, or conscience and at times it seems to be ruling by decree. Washington D.C. is in part responsible for so much of the unrest evident in our country today. By showing preference to one viewpoint over another Washington D.C. automatically inflames the passions of people that share the opposing view. This results in serious division between us. And this results in each group wanting to elect its king to rule over the other group. We must stop attempting to force conformity of opinion, speech, lifestyle acceptance, etc. and once again unite ourselves on the solid ground of the principles of individual freedom based upon the laws of nature and nature's God. I owe you nothing more than to support your individual right to be free, and you owe me that and nothing more. The only entitlement in America is individual freedom.

In the pages and chapters that follow I have identified 11 critical assaults upon our liberty. This is by no means all of the possible ways our freedoms are being eroded but it does, I think, identify and describe some of the most fundamental, critical, and dangerous assaults on our freedom. Freedom of the individual is the only sustainable form of a just government.

One more thought from President Washington. He states that "...the habits of thinking in a free country should inspire caution..." This segues or moves us naturally into the first chapter of the book entitled - Feeling vs. Thinking. We must all care for our great country. The principles of individual freedom offer us the maximum potential for diversity of all individual pursuits of happiness, our personally held opinions and beliefs, differing lifestyles, speech, religion, and any number of personal choices that belong to *We The People*.

Chapter 1

Feeling vs. Thinking

The Assault on Freedom: In a rational world where freedom reigns thoughts through free speech discover truth, but when emotion or feelings take precedence over reason and thinking the truth discovery process shuts down.

Early one morning, during my daughter's elementary school years, I went to her room and stood by her bedside to awaken her. As I did so, she almost immediately and softly proclaimed "I don't feel like going to school today, Dad."

I thought for a moment. "Do you have a fever?"

"No," she said.

"A stomach ache?"

Again, no.

"Chills?" She shook her head. "Well, are you sick in some other way?"

"No, not exactly."

"Then I got an idea." I thought this would make a good teaching moment as well as getting to the bottom of the quandary.

I said, "Well I know you don't feel like going to school, so what do you think you should do about the situation?"

To which she replied, "I guess I think I should go."

Now kids are smart, and at times I think smarter than adults. We all have strong emotional connections with our children and different parenting styles, so please don't misunderstand my point. Children will test the waters of the parents' emotional as well as rational makeup, or more accurately their tendencies regarding each, at least as far as their own children are concerned. In that way, the child learns which method of persuasion or control, emotional or logical, works best and for which parent. If the child ends up as the teacher in the case of "feeling vs. thinking," woe be unto the parents. There will be a battle for control.

This is yet another example of the natural moral law exhibiting its reality and authority. Make no mistake about it, the child is thinking. Had I simply said, "Ok if you don't feel like going" and I stopped there, making the assumption that she didn't feel good, what do you think the outcome would have likely been?

Was my daughter lying? No, absolutely not. I know this because she was honest when directly asked about several types of sicknesses and by her reply when she thought about what she should do. And she simply said "I don't feel like going to school." A perfectly honest and valid statement. How can one be honest while giving two different and opposing answers to the very same situation?

My daughter and I discussed the topic of feeling vs. thinking at length, probably on the ride to school. Thinking and feeling are two entirely different human faculties. Moreover, both are very important to the healthy human experience in life. They are both needed, but they are different. Each can lead you to a very different conclusion over the same matter, issue, or question. There are times in life when both may apply, like in the case above. One can describe the feeling of being sick and also provide a logical explanation of the specific illness. Sometimes one or the other is needed in order to arrive at the logical conclusion. For example, if a husband describes his love to his wife in strictly logical verbiage, aha, he is likely in trouble because logic, in this instance, is not the best choice. Why? Because love is an emotion which contains feeling and passion. An emotion of this type is best conveyed through a response that conveys one's feelings even if those feelings are mostly logic based.

I have watched journalists interview people on serious as well as frivolous subject matters. I can never recall a journalist asking a person what they think about a particular thing. The word "feeling" is almost always the word used in the journalist's question. You may think this a small and perhaps picky point, but I disagree and here is why. I have watched interviews of family members, witnesses of murders, rape, auto crashes, shootings, abortion, and on and on and on. The journalist, in my viewing, invariably asks the person how they "feel" about what happened. As a viewer it would be outrageous to watch the interview, without emotion and compassion for the victims, their families, and friends. "How do you think they feel?" I shout to the reporter on the television—"How do you feel about your wife's rape? How do you feel about the school shooting? How do you feel about a woman's right to choose?" Each of these certainly has an emotional component, but doesn't each of these situations require logic and reason as well?

In the courtroom there is a concept of "leading the witness." The attorney may not do this because it may lead the witness into making a conclusion or claim that the witness may not intend to make. In other words, leading the witness or interviewee is basically manipulation. The same holds true for the journalist interviewing someone, as to the possible manipulated conclusion. For the journalist, however, the way the question is framed is not illegal. So leading the witness or interviewee, may be unethical but it is not illegal. I always hoped and waited for an interviewee to make this distinction, correct the journalist, and tell the journalist what he thinks. Still waiting.

Since motive is a matter of the heart and the heart is hidden from human view, I will not go there. Except to say, that of all the years of journalism school required for the journalist, would this distinction of phraseology or verbiage ever have been a topic of classroom discussion? Would a top journalist know and realize the important difference between a question framed by the word "feeling" and one framed by "thinking?" My guess is yes. Make your own assessment of journalistic political motive or agenda. Keep in mind there are all sorts of national polls and opinion statistics being conducted all the time. If leading of the interviewee is happening, it could lead to wildly misleading data which can then be used to demagogue and sway public opinion. Words have meaning.

Lastly, let's say leading is happening, and it is skewing statistical results, cultural tendencies, and or swaying public opinion one way or other. I am not laying all on the journalist. The person being asked the question also has a responsibility to answer the question with the appropriate human faculty. To select the correct inherent faculty to respond with, lies squarely upon the shoulder of the person answering the question. In logic this type of emotionally-framed question would be in the category of "appeal to emotion." Appeal to emotion is the logical fallacy in which an effort is made to manipulate an emotional response or outcome, instead of a rational and reasoned logical outcome. As we have seen, the two can have a very different result or consequence. A point not to be missed here.

Appeal to emotion is the logical fallacy in which an effort is made to manipulate an emotional response or outcome, instead of a rational and reasoned logical outcome.

Politicians, as well as people peddling dogma or narrative over truth, use this type of logical fallacy in an effort to gain support for an idea or a vote. We see this almost daily in our society. All too often in lieu of introspective and healthy intellectual discourse to arrive at a “truth” of a matter, someone will throw in an emotional ploy to label, categorize, or stigmatize, to shift the audience to an appeal to emotion to win the argument. The idea is to have the audience switch from thinking to feeling, thus hopefully being more easily manipulated to a coerced conclusion.

Our social order through our government or laws, etc. is established on universal absolute natural moral law, reason, and logic, because there could be no just society without absolute universal standards that apply equally to all its citizens. Our nation has not been established upon the quicksand of subjective feelings and emotion. Therefore, when a matter of civil society or government is concerned it does not behoove us to make these judgments on an emotional feeling plane but rather a logical thinking one.

Consider: A demagogic dishonest person and his opponent, a generally honest and respected person, are both seeking to be elected. Two very different states are up for grabs in the election. The first state is a mostly emotional people, highly susceptible to charismatic persuasion and less reliant on logic and truthful information. The second state is the opposite. The majority of its people are more bent toward reason, logic, and they tend to be informed. Which state favors whom? Obviously, the dishonest demagogue would prefer the first state. His election in the latter or second state would be more difficult. Over time, which state do you think would more likely end up with corrupt scoundrels or even a tyrant in charge of the government? Which state do you think would have more honest science, businesses, government, and less social problems? Lastly, which type of state or society do you think is best for us? It is dangerous to walk around unarmed—we must inform ourselves and think.

Decades ago I first heard journalists asking questions that obviously required the faculty of reason or thinking but being framed in the context of "emotion." Now with the pervasive movement of political correctness, which is based upon emotion, I can't help but wonder if there is a direct correlation. But I am more concerned with political correctness and its companion social justice, as a major destructive and truth-evading and enslaving force that needs our thoughtful attention.

> *Political correctness and social justice advocates seek to establish their own moral codes.*

Political correctness is a philosophy or movement that seeks to displace by force, coercion, labeling, ridicule, etc. the philosophy of reasoned truth which is based on observable, rationally discernible, absolute, universal natural moral law, with the philosophy of an arbitrary, subjective system led by "emotion" or "feeling" absent any universal standard. Political correctness and social justice advocates seek to establish their own moral codes. It is not logical that two distinct separate bodies of natural moral law exist - thus one is an impostor. This politically correct contrived moral code is highly subjective, arbitrary, hyper emotional, rapidly and constantly mutating, truth-evading, and without universal standards. Therefore, it is unstable and dangerously prone to taking society down a path of erroneous or false moral conclusions. A P.C. path which has and will continue to have terrible and destructive consequences against our individual rights as well as our society in general. It is built upon emotion and vice as evidenced by the actions of most of its participants, and therefore unfit to be a part of any civil system. Consider this, when someone does not agree or like your view on a matter, any matter, and then proceeds to name call, ridicule, or label you with pejorative labels instead of attempting to defeat or refute your view on a calm rational and reasoned intellectual basis, there is a problem. This is the first sign that something is amiss. Truth does not seek the cover of darkness for that is the role of the lie. Political correctness is a destructive force by design regardless of the intent. I do not care to argue, at this juncture, the intent anymore than I need, or wish to argue the origin of the existence of natural moral law. I am concerned here with what is presently occurring. Both concepts, motive, and

> *Truth does not seek the cover of darkness for that is the role of the lie.*

origin, are moot to the point of practical application and import of this negative force upon civil society.

In 1776 Thomas Paine said, “He that will promote discord, under a government so equally formed as this would have joined Lucifer in his revolt.” A recent U.S. President and the National Education Association (NEA) recommended a book about creating social unrest which was written by the social and political radical, Saul Alinsky, to the nation's public school teachers - as a classroom aid. Alinsky dedicated his book, *Rules for Radicals*, to Lucifer.

In 1776 Thomas Paine said, “He that will promote discord, under a government so equally formed as this would have joined Lucifer in his revolt.”

I want to include a few examples of the impact political correctness has already had upon our society. Let’s first look at profiling. Profiling is a good and very useful tool for selecting candidates for a particular objective. For example, academic profiling aids universities in establishing standards that a university expects its candidates to achieve in order to be considered for admissions. Criminal profiling enables police departments to build profiles of certain criminals in order to effect their speedy arrest and thereby help maintain the safety of the public. None of this is really any different from any corporation, government, or other employer setting standards for a particular job they may be seeking to fill. Building a profile is simply a way to establish and strive for certain honest “standards.” That’s it, and it’s a good thing.

In A Response to Cato's Fourth through Seventh Letters, Thomas Paine said, "He who dares not offend cannot be honest."

Along comes the politically correct and social-justice-thought police who demagogue profiling, claiming it offensive and racially discriminatory. I must add here that the public has a responsibility to not go along or participate in this system that demagogues or emotionalizes issues rather than seeks truth through thought and reason in issues that are important to society. Academic, criminal, terrorist, and employment profiling is now reframed and simply said to be "racial profiling." Each category of standards is removed, be it academic, terrorism-related national security, or criminal investigations. The sport-loving public would not tolerate, for a second, the removal of standards of recruitment for athletes in the NBA, NFL, Baseball, College Sports, etc. Why? Because they intuitively know that this would destroy the highly exciting competitive nature of the games. It would lower the standard of play and thereby destroy the game. Why then is this allowed where it really matters to the survival of our society and country? Can one not easily, from that sports analogy, conclude that political correctness and social justice is thus destroying our historically high-achieving country and lowering our standards as a nation? In the sports world example, would the person implementing politically correct standards in the

Thomas Paine said, "He who dares not offend cannot be honest."

NBA, for example, be thought of as trying to help or harm the game?

The answer is obvious but if he, perchance, said he was trying to help he would be dismissed as an incompetent, don't you think? Yet we tolerate this in larger society based, apparently, upon not wanting to hurt some one's feelings. This has happened because the general American public is caring in nature, in my view, thus not wanting to hurt anyone's feelings. Therefore, we are feeling our way rather than thinking our way through many of these issues. Perhaps too many in the public don't see a connection between the political correctness movement and the destructive impact it is having upon their lives, culture, and government. This is unfortunate because there is a very fundamental nexus between the founding principles of this nation and the destructive force of political correctness upon those principles. Political correctness, whether intentionally or not, is a direct assault upon our founding principles and our culture in general. Our survival as a free people is at stake, and much hallowed ground of freedom has already been lost in this regard. The political correctness (cultural Marxism) crowd is always looking for a wedge, it would seem. An America based in reason and natural law will defend individual

An America based in reason and natural law will defend individual liberty and freedom, but an America based in emotion and moral subjectivism will destroy it.

liberty and freedom, but an America based in emotion and moral subjectivism will destroy it. They were not happy with the racial ratios that resulted from setting standards so they found a way to emotionalize and reframe the issue and have the standards removed. Now all types of profiling have the same political correctness label. Any profiling, now simply called "racial profiling," is said to be discrimination and has been made illegal. This has the effect of removing qualifying standards and truth-seeking, and shifting the focus squarely upon race or other non-standard standards. That was not the case before.

Selecting people upon the basis of race is now the norm in many areas. The lunacy here is that now there truly is racism in these issues due to political correctness and it is enforced by law. The subtle perversion and irony of the argument that profiling is discriminatory and then forcing a system of legally mandated discrimination upon the public is truly maddening. However, on the bright side it is very revealing of the people behind the movement. It is either deception, or ignorance of the highest order.

We have and are replacing the merit system of standards, based in natural law with the arbitrary, standardless system of politically correct behavior and speech codes or rules. Reason will tell you that the objective of attempting to placate people's feelings instead seeking truth of any matter through reason and logic is largely to blame for the decline of Western society and culture. The stated goal of cultural Marxism is to cause the decline of the

West and Western culture. My objective here is not to prove a correlation between the stated goal of cultural Marxists and the clear consequence of a society led by a political correctness and social justice culture of feeling. But rather to state the obvious, that there is a clear similarity between the stated goals of political correctness, social justice, and cultural Marxism, and the decline of our national and societal standards.

In addition to the issue of profiling there are many more politically correct terms and codes to know or be aware of.

Jazz Hands is a politically correct notion that traditional clapping may be an emotional trigger to some individuals and therefore emotionally upsetting or harmful.[1] The politically correct solution is to have the audience silently wave their hands over their heads instead of clapping. I have a question—How is it known that waving one's hands in the air is not emotionally triggering to someone else? Perhaps someone was spanked as a child and the hand waving could be a trigger to the memory of the parental spanking hand. Could this not be emotionally harmful? Hey, I'm just trying to help.

Micro-aggression is a politically correct idea that there are forms of "subconscious racism."[2] That is right. Subconscious racism, is racism a person engages in and is not even aware of it. An example or two: "America is the land of opportunity," "Where are you from?" "I believe the most qualified person should get the job." See if you can spot the subconscious micro-aggression in the prior examples. Then go online and check your answers.

Trigger Warnings are verbal warnings that are spoken before a professor or speaker begins to speak on a topic that may cause an emotionally upsetting reaction in someone who may be listening.[3] Try to imagine the impossibility and ridiculousness of this application in any practical real life setting.

Banned Books are all too common as well. Many classic books have been banned from the classroom because their content is said to be emotionally upsetting to some people. Here are a few examples: *Adventures of Huckleberry Finn* by Mark Twain 1884, *Gone With The Wind* by Margaret Mitchell 1936, *For Whom the Bell Tolls* by Ernest Hemmingway 1940, *Moby-Dick* by Herman Melville 1851.[4]

There are examples of a person of one race choosing to identify as another race. Some people of one sex "identify" as another sex. Some people are simply and arbitrarily deciding what "their" truth is. One can't help but wonder where this will lead next. Suppose an individual proclaims to "identify" as an airline pilot or the leader of a nation when he clearly is not. Should the "emotionally identifying" pilot be allowed to fly a commercial jet? Should the person that identifies himself as a head of state be treated as if he really were - out of respect for his feelings of course. If he is not allowed, in either case, should he then be able to legally sue for discrimination?

Perhaps we should demand that any politically correct President accept the emotionally identifying head of state at a televised state dinner at the White House. I'd love to watch the show and the lunacy of the make believe on display. Imagine if either scenario was denied, would this then be discrimination of some sort? What would it be? I'll tell you what it would be. It would be turning the tables on political correctness and cultural Marxism by pitting itself against itself just as it has so cunningly positioned our society via the logical fallacy of appeal to emotion. The politically correct President would then become the court jester in his own kingdom of political correctness and social justice. Now of course this is absurd. I only make it to expose the fallacious insanity of the politically correct movement and the societal acquiescence to it. It does, however, make a very clarifying point of exposing the idiocy of what is happening. To be clear—Would any politically correct or social justice advocating President accept the "Identifying Head of State" (IDHOS) for an evening of pretense, or would he reject such a notion risking the exposure of the fraud he is involved in? We have no choice but to resist and abandon this destructive nonsense or be destroyed by it ourselves.

If someone wants to live his or her life in this pathos of feeling, he or she has that right as an individual. My resistance to the political correctness issue lies in the legal forcing of society to participate. You cannot be said to be upholding the rights of an individual when, at the same time you are forcing a paradigm upon others thereby trampling their rights to have a different view. The subjectivity of truth is the denial of truth itself because if truth is only subjective then there is no truth at all. If nothing can be truly learned, then there are no such things as universal standards, and therefore no basis whatever for law and justice. Government then becomes arbitrary and illegitimate. Eventual chaos and societal breakdown will be the result. Therefore, it is my reasoned observation that the subjectivity of truth is the only falsehood evident in this entire scenario.

"There are two ways to be fooled. One is to believe what is not true; the other is to refuse to accept what is true." Soren Kierkegaard

"There are two ways to be fooled. One is to believe what is not true; the other is to refuse to accept what is true." Soren Kierkegaard

Let me be very clear. I have no intention to ever ridicule anyone who may have any form of PTSD or any other life trauma or other induced fear, phobia, anxiety, whether racial, sexual, or otherwise. I say the same to someone who simply has a different view than I, no matter how strange or weird I may think his idea. All people have a right to their beliefs, period. Also, I am not speaking to those legitimate issues where people may be truly hurting or suffering in any way. I would always encourage any suffering individual to seek the appropriate professional help and that of loved ones and friends. Moreover, I do not advocate ridiculing anyone in order to belittle, force conformity, to harm, or harass them in any way. We are all human beings here and we all need support, love, and help at some points in our lives.

I am, however, talking about the politically correct cultural Marxist tactics and methods that are so obviously used to stifle debate, emotionalize and demagogue issues, and act as a generally destructive force in this society. I do not have to choose, nor will I be forced, to suspend my faculty of reason to pursue truth in all matters of life as it pertains to me and my participation in my own life, culture, and country. In other words, no one can be forced to participate in a paradigm they "think" is false, illogical, and destructive and runs contrary to their right of conscience. The real and serious problem is that political correctness has already forced itself into our police departments, military, government, national security, schools, churches, and just about every institution in this nation. Interestingly enough this is, again, eerily similar to the stated goals of cultural Marxists to bring down the west by infiltrating and destructively criticizing every institution. Do your own research on political correctness and social justice origins, cultural Marxism, and the Frankfurt School. A couple of names to help you get started are Antonio Gramsci, founder of Italian communism, and Georg Lukacs, one of the founders of western Marxism. Have a look at Marxists.org and you will find more socialist and Marxist material than you may care to read.

Additionally, it is important to recognize that the socialist, statist, cultural Marxist revolution exists, is real, is a process of destruction not construction, and it is ongoing, not a one-time battle or event. This process has been happening in the United States since at least 1913 when the era of big government progressivism began in earnest. No American alive today lives in and experiences the freedom granted by our Constitution and enjoyed by our founders and other earlier Americans. American freedom enjoyed by our ancestors and our Founders has not been experienced in this country for more than one hundred years. This includes free market capitalism which none of us have ever experienced. We have a system of socialized, regulated commerce, but more on these issues in other chapters. The only point here is that the political correctness movement with its emphasis on feelings and emotion instead of open calm intellectual reasoned debate or discourse is not new nor is it the only method being employed by the statist progressives to build bigger statist government. A man who fears open discourse is a man who fears truth.

A man who fears open discourse is a man who fears truth.

The political correctness intellectual sleight of hand has the country, in many ways, emoting instead of thinking. We are supposed to be a nation of laws built upon natural law and the principles gleaned thereof. Universal natural law offers every individual the protection afforded by his own personally and privately held individual rights. The political correctness movement has the nation on an emotional track in an attempt, I think, to increase the chances that America will unsuspectingly and unintentionally trade in her principled-based individual rights and thus freedom, by accepting non-principled subjective arbitrary rules of behavior or political correctness code book. The potential for this to happen is very real. This is evidenced by the level of political correctness codes already being employed within our military, federal, and local law enforcement, federal, and local government, terrorism efforts, halls of academia, etc.

The political correctness movement must fight its battles on the battlefield of feeling because it cannot win upon the battlefield of thinking.

The political correctness movement must fight its battles on the battlefield of feeling because it cannot win upon the battlefield of thinking.

Therefore, it must demagogue the issues and viciously attack its opponents with pejorative name-calling and labeling. Political correctness is based upon emotion and vice, and therefore it must keep the game on the emotional and emotionally divisive level. It also will venomously attack anyone attempting to have a thoughtful discussion based upon reason and logic. Look and see if you can find your own examples of this taking place. You can if you will but look.

There are many age-old arguments and one such age-old argument is absolutism vs. subjectivism or relativism. In other words, universal discoverable truths (absolutism) vs. no universal discoverable truth (relativism/subjectivism). Our country, and your freedom, is based upon absolutism in natural law. The founding patriots rebelled against the subjectivism of the kings, queens, dictators, and tyrants of the old world and won. The political correctness movement is an attempt to return to the past. This movement is based upon subjectivism wrapped in emotional arguments, not thoughtful intellectual arguments grounded in reason. If there are no universal rules or principles, then the ruling authority can simply make up the rules as it desires just like the kings of old and that was the tyranny our forefathers fought to the death over. The tyranny that chopped off heads rather than risk any threat to its authority by open and rational discourse. That tyranny chopped off heads because it was offended by someone's speech. That tyranny was what the American Patriots rightly rebelled against knowing it was either victory or the chopping block.

The political correctness movement is more serious and dangerous to our nation's survival than many people believe. Our nation is being attacked and potentially transformed at the level of our founding principles, but the battle innocuously appears to be upon a more superficial or non-critical level. Failing to recognize this is a deadly mistake. For example, the transgender bathroom issue and or the gender pronoun issue are more than just what bathroom or pronoun one should use. Any solution must protect the rights of conscience of all involved. The bathroom or pronoun is the battlefield but the principle of right of conscience is what is being attacked. And this should be a matter of concern for all Americans, whether, gay, straight, transgender, Christian, atheist, or whatever. In other words, to legally force all to use the same bathroom or arbitrary subjective pronoun tramples the rights of some under the pretense of protecting the rights of others. This is an assault at the fundamental and principle level of each American's right of conscience. Some people may not care who is in the bathroom with them while others care deeply about who is there with them or their children. Therefore, any constitutional solution must protect the rights of all while denying the rights of none. Here is the real issue—none of us can constitutionally force our opinion upon another much less force one or the other to comply with that opinion with the force of law. Subjectivism vs. absolutism. Absolutism protects all while subjectivism does not. Absolutism in natural moral law is freedom for each one of us. Subjectivism is tyranny and bondage for each one of us by the dictator-like behavior of one over another.

This nation was founded upon many principles, not the least of which are the principles of sound reasoning and respect for each individual's God-given individual rights. The right to be free and live your life according to the dictates of your own conscience. The right of each man's conscience must be respected or the right of all men's consciences is in peril. This is also why the role of government has no place in private matters of opinion or rights of conscience. These matters belong to the people and their respective states per the Constitution. A just government by consent of "We the people," in America was formed to protect us from trampling the rights of another and at the same time constrain the same government from trampling the rights of any of us. The American form of government places the government at the footstool of man and not the other way around. Government, you are not our king, but "We the people" are yours.

> *Government, you are not our king, but "We the people" are yours.*

As a nation, we have before us a Faustian bargain of tyrannical magnitude between feeling vs. thinking. The Faustian bargain before us threatens our freedom by the: 1) tool of emotion, 2) as an example, the bathroom as the method, case, or vessel in order to 3) fundamentally transform, damage, or remove the right of conscience for all. While people are chatting about a bathroom, legally enforced pronoun usage, and using the law to force a baker to bake a wedding cake, the right of conscience is what is being assaulted here and I believe that to be the goal. To some these bathroom, pronoun, and wedding cake arguments may seem superficial or silly but much is at stake on the level of principle. An attempt is being made to fundamentally transform this nation. Fundamental transformation is not about the wedding cake, bathroom or what pronoun a person prefers to be called, it is about the principle of right of conscience.

The erosion of the many moral traditional manners of society has sadly given way to an imposter known as political correctness and social justice. Basic values of kindness and respect for others have, in too many instances, caved in to the tireless taskmaster of the political correctness rule book. There is no peace in this. It is a false philosophy of the false gods of outcome in fairness and equality, built upon the mushy and illusive foundation of subjectivity of emotion. Just look at the uproar and friction it has caused in the bathroom issue alone. Again, there is no peace in this. Our founding principles are being attacked by having us argue over their application. We must regain the concepts of our founding principles and not allow ourselves to be divided by our varying opinions. Division of opinion is in part the beauty of America. Division of opinion based upon unity of the principles of freedom is the hallmark of America. Where there is love of fellowman, mutual respect, and tolerance, truth is honored and our nation, its people, and its good cause of freedom are advanced.

Division of opinion based upon unity of the principles of freedom is the hallmark of America. Where there is love of fellowman, mutual respect, and tolerance, truth is honored and our nation, its people, and its good cause of freedom are advanced.

We must as a nation return to the values of moral virtues and thoughtfully, peacefully, and constitutionally resolve the issues before us. We must have respect for those with whom we disagree. Matters of opinion and conscience do not belong in the hands of the law. We are being played against ourselves, in part, by our own government because, I think, we have forgotten our founding principles and the history of tyranny from which our forefathers saved themselves and freely granted to us. We as a society must return to the proper use of both of the faculties of feeling and thinking girded by the principles of absolutism of natural moral law.

Children first use emotion to achieve their desires, but adults eventually turn to thought!

The Takeaway for Freedom's Defense: Emotion will often accept what reason would reject—therefore, put emotion aside in matters where reason is required.

Chapter 2

The Right of Conscience

The Assault on Freedom: Legally forcing someone to act in accordance with or acceptance of another's belief contrary to his or her own, is an assault against the constitutional individual right of conscience. This un-American action has the effect of turning a man's mind against himself.

> "I have sworn upon the altar of God eternal hostility against every form of tyranny over the mind of man."
>
> Thomas Jefferson in a letter to Benjamin Rush
> from Monticello, September 23, 1800

> "Security under our Constitution is given to the rights of conscience and private judgment. They are by nature subject to no control but that of Deity (The Lord), and in that the free situation they are now left."
>
> John Jay, First Chief Justice of the Supreme Court [5]

> "Government is instituted to protect property of every sort......Conscience is the most sacred of all property."
>
> James Madison, Fourth President of the United States [6]

Conscience—that innate and innermost aspect of our being that acts as our personal guidance or control system. The human conscience is the central essence of our very being. Nature and nature's God have placed the natural moral law within each human mind. That part of our being aids us in the making of value judgment of the rightness or wrongness of a matter. And in so doing one's conscience aids the individual in determining and developing his or her belief system. All men have a belief system because all men believe in something. For the man who rejects this notion in favor of believing in nothing at all, point made. I am of the opinion that all men have a religion, for what is religion if not a belief of one's world view. Dictionary.com defines it this way: Religion; "a set of beliefs concerning the cause, nature, and purpose of the universe, especially when considered as the creation of a superhuman agency or agencies, usually involving devotional and ritual observances, and often containing a moral code governing the conduct of human affairs." Alternately Dictionary.com says: "something one believes in and follows devotedly; a point or matter of ethics or conscience...."

One's conscience is that part of one's essence that aids and enables man to formulate his beliefs which permeate his complete individual existence.

Men universally and cross culturally generally agree upon most matters of right and wrong such as stealing, murder, lying, and harming or intruding upon another's property or interest. But the scope of human conscience moves beyond these types of value judgments and into such areas as religion, lifestyle, sexuality, politics, etc. These are the areas in which men primarily have differing views of conscience. One's conscience is that part of one's essence that aids and enables man to formulate his beliefs which permeate his complete individual existence. Beliefs which we all have a right to freely establish within ourselves and to remain constant in these beliefs or to cultivate them or evolve our beliefs without coercion from man or state.

All men have a right to their consciences. For what is a human being if not his conscience? What has a man if not his mind? His ideas about himself and his world belong to him alone and by extension can only be altered or changed by him. No man has a right to another man's mind. In this matter man is subject only to God, if one believes in God.

No man has a right to another man's mind.

Thomas Jefferson said, "No provision in our constitution ought to be dearer to man than that which protects the rights of conscience against the enterprise of the civil authority."[7]

Imagine not being able to live out your life according to your own thoughts and beliefs. Instead you are forced by the state to bend to another's will. If all men are equal in their humanity, and we are, and all men have a conscience and beliefs of their own, as each does, then what authority does one human being have to legally force his conscience's desire upon another human being?

He has none. I speak here of legal force or coercion of one's conscience. I am not speaking of natural discourse freely engaged in by people of similar or varying opinions for the purpose of persuasion and or intellectual engagement. Another question: What type of personality would seek the force of law to accomplish this aim against a fellow human being? Last question: Would this action to stifle another man's belief's through speech be of the spirit of vice or of the spirit of virtue?

Consider the following. In your mind's eye, picture yourself at a gathering of many people all together having a good time. Now picture someone at the gathering insisting that everyone must agree with him on a certain matter of religion, politics, sexuality, global warming, or the like. Assume this person is relentless and refuses to stop until all agree with him. He claims to be deeply offended by the others' opposing views. The person is unable to persuade any to his way of thinking and leaves the gathering in a fury. He later returns with a legal document. This person has political connections and was able to persuade the government to enact a law forbidding any views differing from his, as he was previously insisting. It is now a reality that the gatherers, as word of the legal document begins to spread, have become somewhat subdued. Conversations become blander and less specific and therefore more superficial. A modicum of fear sets in as no one desires to be held in violation of the new speech law. A notable absence of that spirit of liberty and spontaneity exists, and perhaps honesty of discourse.

There is less smiling, less laughter. People begin to leave now, as if to escape the growing heavy mood.

In the following days there are reports circulating of arrests and fines due to violations of the new law. Fear begins to spread through the land, especially among those who know they hold an opposing view of that now upheld by the state. Honest open discourse is among the first casualties, as is truth. Truth does not depart the land because no man has authority to make it do so. Truth exists upon its own authority independent of the prevailing winds of opinion. Truth does not hide, but it is hidden by men in fear to speak, as well as men in fear of speech. Why? Because too many love their lives and selves more than truth. Sadly, this will aid in the possible rise of tyranny in the land as it has for centuries. Never hold anything above the mantle of truth. Seek truth in life in all matters great and small.

> *Truth exists upon its own authority independent of the prevailing winds of opinion.*

You may be tempted to dismiss the above as an overly whimsical fantasy with no basis in reality. If you had this thought, you might take it as a sure sign you need to read history and brush up on current events. I try to do this myself. The present world and history is filled with kings, queens, dictators, and tyrants as well as big government advocating statists or progressives, that have done exactly what the above scenario describes and much, much, worse.

The tyrants of the past used informants to report dissidents to the crown. There was no right of conscience in speech or belief and men were hunted like animals for daring to have their own thoughts. Independent thinking was a threat to the king or authority. Keep this in mind.

King Henry VIII instituted the Act of Supremacy in 1534. He declared himself as King to be the Supreme Head of the Church of England. Many Catholics were executed under his rule. The executions, for holding and believing one's own thoughts, under Henry the VIII are estimated to be a high as 72,000 people.

"Bloody Mary" (Queen Mary I), daughter of King Henry VIII, ruled England from 1553-1558. In less than five years Bloody Mary burned over 300+ Protestants at the stake for the charge of "heresy." Heresy is holding a belief that runs contrary to the ruling authority. Bloody Mary sought to reunite England with the Church of Rome and she did not want any resistance from the people, especially the Protestants. She, therefore, instilled the fear of the Crown throughout the land. Especially to those who held beliefs according to their consciences, that differed from the state, which was the Queen "Bloody" Mary. She condemned her cousin Lady Jane Grey to death by fire at the stake. She also condemned Thomas Cranmer, Archbishop of Canterbury, to be burned at the stake as well. More than one person was burned to death at the stake for daring to have their own thoughts and beliefs for every week of Bloody Mary's reign. Would this make you afraid to have and speak your own thoughts?

In 1593 Elizabeth I enacted the Act Against Puritans. Puritans were made to conform to the Church of England or forfeit all property and to depart the realm. Refusal meant the death penalty. It is estimated that over 200 people were executed, simply because of what they believed, under the rule of Elizabeth I.

King James of England came to the throne in 1603. The Puritans made requests of King James to provide some separation between the church and the state. King James, a believer in the Divine Right of Kings, became angered at this and the Crown began to pursue dissenters. Puritans were hunted and persecuted because they dared to believe differently than the King. A small band of Pilgrims, including William Bradford, began meeting at Scrooby Mansion in Nottinghamshire, England. They later fled to Leiden Holland because Holland was the only republic at the time. This group of pilgrims eventually came to America. The story of the early pilgrim's plight prior to America is fascinating, harrowing, and truly inspiring.

The Thirty Years War, 1618-1648, began when the Holy Roman Empire tried to enforce uniformity of belief upon Europe. Seven to eight million people were killed.

King Louis XIV of France believed in absolutism of the crown and thus declared: "L'etat, C'est Moi!" (The state is me!) King Louis XIV believed in the divine right of kings. He believed He was the direct representative of God. He revoked the Edict of Nantes which granted certain rights to French Huguenots (Protestants). He then instilled the Edict of Fontainebleau. With this he had all Protestant Churches destroyed, dissolved all Protestant marriages, forbade Protestants from gathering together, closed all Protestant schools, and expelled all Protestant clergy. He reigned from 1643 -1715.

The previous tidbits of the history of tyranny do not even begin to scratch the surface. Tyranny occurred, and continues to occur, in all parts of the world. Each time the Monarchy changed hands, the laws changed. For a time, the Catholics were hunted and executed, at other times it would be the Protestants or whatever philosophy or belief the monarchy or state held at the time. The point here is that the monarchy, not the church, decided the law of the realm even though at times the two were seemingly united. The monarchy did, however, act in the name of the church. The Crown existed by law and deadly force. The church existed in part by permission and consent of the Crown. Make no mistake about it, the Crown or state ultimately controlled the church. This distinction is a profound one and must be understood accurately because it became an important pillar in the later founding of America.

The Pilgrims were deadly familiar with the danger of combining the church and state as one authoritative force. They knew very well the bondage and perils of life under the sole authority of the state. Tyranny of conscience by the state is why the Pilgrims fled England in the first place. That is also why in the Mayflower Compact they took great measure to avoid having themselves put back under the same governmental bondage of denial of conscience they came from. They also avoided putting anyone else under the bondage and tyranny of state-controlled matters of conscience. No one was forced, coerced, pressured, or otherwise made to convert to Christianity in order to sign the Mayflower Compact.

In the Old World the governmental power was structured as God-above-King, and at times it seemed King-above-God, and then the people being ruled beneath. In their wisdom the Pilgrims changed this order to God, people, and then the king or government. This was the very early beginning of the people controlling the state rather than the state controlling the people. This was the beginning of government by consent of the people being governed—self-government.

Clarity in understanding the difference in this order is paramount. To understand the historic event that was the founding of America and the American Constitution one must fully grasp this paradigm shift of man controlling government instead of government controlling man. Man does not control or rule man in any manner, religious, governmental, or otherwise. Man has no authority to rule over another man without consent. A just and legitimate government is by consent of the governed only. Only

God, if one believes, is over man. No one was, therefore, forced to believe in any particular God or religion even though Christianity was the dominant belief for the Pilgrims. The notion that all men are equal in their humanity was brought to America, by the Christians. This is a matter of historical fact. This philosophical, Christian, and legal breakthrough in the structure of civil government was the true beginning of freedom in the New World. Freedom of conscience to all no matter what your personal beliefs happen to be. Would it not take some person or a group of people with a very high moral sensitivity to truth, love, virtue, and absolute moral principle, to establish in law and government that all men are equal in their humanity, no matter their personal beliefs or lifestyle? No king, queen, dictator, tyrant, statist, or progressive would ever do such a thing—and never has. It would be against his own interest of self-appointed arbitrary rule. Yet, the statist has, in many ways, created the illusion that the churchman or Christian in government is the greatest threat.

Think about that for while. The church man may want to peacefully persuade you to a different view, but it is the king, queen, dictator, tyrant or statist/progressive that wants to force you by law to a different view.

Let's now move forward to the year 1926 and the Prohibition Era (alcohol beverages were banned by the US government) is in full swing. This was the early years of the progressive big government era as well. People desiring to be free and have a drink if they chose, found ways around the laws. Sale of bootleg alcohol was booming. Much of it made of industrial alcohol.

Christmas Eve, snowy and cold, a man comes stammering into New York's Bellevue Hospital. He was in great fear of "Santa Claus". Before the medical personnel could determine what was wrong with him, he died. The cause, murder, or was it alcohol poisoning. So what killed him?

Later it was determined the U.S. Government was not happy with the results of the prohibition laws, as people continued to drink and speakeasies thrived, so they resorted to poisoning the alcohol. The United States Government ordered all industrial alcohol poisoned and they placed no warning label. Seymour M. Lowman, Assistant Secretary of Treasury later said of the fringes that continued to drink are "dying off fast from poison hooch."[8] If this results in a sober America "a good job will have been done." Total deaths from the U.S. Government poisoning operation is estimated to be in excess of 10,000 people, with some estimates as high as 50,000. Well, the government at least got its message across, right? The end justifies the means. The sacrifice of the one for the many for the greater good of all. Oh, that was Karl Marx's idea.

This is a prime example of why the group think of socialism, communism, or similar is wrong, evil, and dangerous. Individuals matter, those poisoned individuals, for the Marxist communist idea of the greater good or supposed good of the group, by the U.S.

Government, matter. This is why America is the land of freedom where individual rights reign. Why? Because each and every one of us matters. Why? Because we are human individuals. Socialism and communist thought ignores the individual in favor of the group.

In their Communist Manifesto, Karl Marx and Frederick Engels said, "And the abolition of this state of things is called by the bourgeois, abolition of individuality and freedom! And rightly so. The abolition of bourgeois individuality, bourgeois independence, and bourgeois freedom is undoubtedly aimed at."[9] And they continued later in the document, "You must, therefore, confess that by 'individual' you mean no other person than the bourgeois, than the middle-class owner of property. This person must, indeed, be swept out of the way, and made impossible."[10]

The communal link between the governmental structures of kings, queens, dictators, tyrants, and modern day statists or progressives is rooted in the same big-government tree.

The communal link between the governmental structures of kings, queens, dictators, tyrants, and modern day statists or progressives is rooted in the same big-government tree. Each one is a slightly different branch and that is the only difference. All of them believe in the power of the state over the individual. All of them have engaged in whatever means necessary to gain power over the individual. This includes, killing people for their beliefs, deceit, lying, making your life difficult by regulation of your affairs and property whether private or public. This information is available to anyone who cares to take a peek. Take a peek!

In 2015, while speaking at the South by Southwest Technology Conference, Al Gore suggests that we should punish climate-change deniers.[11] Al Gore, it would appear, wants to deny your right of conscience to disagree with global warming.

In 2014, during an interview with climatedepot.com, Robert F. Kennedy Jr. speaking of climate change (global warming) skeptics "I think its treason...do I think they should be in jail - I think they should be enjoying three hots and a cot at The Hague with all the other war criminals."[12] Robert F. Kennedy Jr. appears to want to deny the right of conscience to disagree with global warming.

Before leaving the topic of tyranny in this discussion of right of conscience, there is a little more history that is vital to understand. I think that understanding what I am about to say will enable you to connect the dots to the seemingly disparate, vicious, and relentless assaults on all aspects of our Western and American culture. I think understanding this will open one's eyes to the fundamental transformation that is underway in our land. But you need to do your own research. I will only give a brief account here, so I really encourage you to dig into these topics yourself.

The *Frankfurt School* located in Germany dates back to the 1920s. The Frankfurt School is a think-tank of socialism and its companion communism. Its primary mission is to destroy the West. The Frankfurt school developed a theory called "Critical Theory." The theory basically consists of destructive criticism of all things Western. Destructive criticism of Christianity, marriage, traditions of the west, family, American culture, church, individual rights, American exceptionalism, schools, natural moral law, American Constitution, race relations, and so on.

The idea is to use the constant clamor of relentless destructive criticism in every aspect of western culture from its roots, founding, and onward. Destructive criticism of perceived or real inequities without ever offering a positive solution or participating in a rational discussion on the matter. Why? Because the goal is to destroy western culture and America as the titular head. To use America's open society against itself. To create division upon division, crack upon crack, opinion against opinion, until we crumble into chaos.

The antidote to the progressive politics of division is to love and respect each other and each person's rights to conscience of thought and speech.

The antidote to the progressive politics of division is to love and respect each other and each person's rights to conscience of thought and speech. A polite society will be open to criticism and thereby vulnerable to destruction by aggressive, never-ending negative criticism with force. Look around and you will no doubt find examples of this destructive cultural force. It is a movement to empower the state over the individual by destroying western Constitutional freedom. I suggest you conduct an Internet search on college campus politics and free speech, for example. There are now safe zones where one is safe from hearing opposing views of another's conscience. There are free speech zones on some campuses. Has no one told these universities that America is a free speech zone? The political correctness street preachers of tolerance and diversity enjoy their free speech while they reject, shout down, and refuse tolerance and diversity of intellectual discourse and the conscience opinions of others. There is only one way, and that is the politically correct way. Is this not shockingly ironic coming from those who have preached tolerance and diversity for all these years?

*America **IS** a free speech zone*

The *Frankfurt School* is where political correctness and multiculturalism have their roots. They are part of the destructive criticism concept to destroy western culture. It is called cultural Marxism. There exists a notion known as the long march through western culture to the destruction of the west.

What is this? The long march through western culture is known as the emersion of cultural Marxism throughout every aspect of western culture and using destructive criticism to destroy it. The term long march denotes this is to be a gradual, relentless, never ending effort to tear down western culture. This is heavy stuff so do not take my word for it. Please research this topic and educate yourself in this area. Your freedom may very well depend upon your doing so.

Free speech is a part of your right of conscience. You have the right to speak your thoughts just as you have a right to think them. It is, nevertheless, a reality that within the world of political correctness (cultural Marxism) free speech is under threat. Of the many ways the PC (political correctness) advocates attempt to limit speech, one is through the notion of being offended. This is being expressed in many ways. The concept is basically that the offended person is able to shut down debate or speech simply by claiming to be terribly emotionally offended. Since offending someone by what you say has traditionally been a moral and cultural no-no in America, this tactic has, thus far, been an effective tool of the Marxist and his long march for purposeful destruction of our culture. In a polite society, the offended immediately gains the upper political and emotional hand in most cases. The then supposed offending speech is labeled politically incorrect and sometimes coupled with the force of law or a part of a larger speech code. The offender is labeled a racist, bigot, intolerant, etc. And on and on the long march through western American culture goes. A man who knows he has the weaker argument, morally, intellectually, and logically, and is not seeking truth as the outcome, will quickly take flight to PC cover to avoid being exposed in his fallacy. What better cover than to appeal to the logical fallacy of emotion and scream and shout and chant and ridicule and condemn and label and categorize and take on the pretense of being victimized. This very thing is a testament to the truth of America as she was founded, and a testament to the absolute fear that the political correctness Marxist culture has toward that truth. They cower in fear of the exposure that would occur if they dared have a fair and rational discourse or debate of ideas in the intellectual arena. An honest debate with reason not emotion reigning supreme. Cowards of truth all!

Ralph Waldo Emerson said, "Let me never fall into the vulgar mistake of dreaming that I am persecuted whenever I am contradicted."

Ralph Waldo Emerson said, "Let me never fall into the vulgar mistake of dreaming that I am persecuted whenever I am contradicted."

Free speech is a central pillar of America's founding therefore the political correctness advocates would have little success demanding that free speech be completely eradicated in principle. Thus they have come up with a different approach which, if it continues, may end up with the same result. The following is my observation and thoughts on the matter. They are doing this by targeting specific examples of free speech and labeling persons as racists, bigoted, etc., in order to assault the principle of free speech. They are implementing the tactic of cultural Marxism.

Let us imagine the principle of free speech in the form of a pie. Now, let's segment the pie into eight pieces. One piece we will call offensive hate speech, so that piece gets removed. Another we call offensive racist speech, so another piece gets removed. Yet another is called offensive to minorities speech, so that slice is removed. Yet another is called climate denier speech, so that piece gets removed. There are way too many political correctness rules to list but you get the point. Before long you don't have much of a pie (speech) left and therefore no principle of free speech. They are going after the whole pie one slice at a time. If authority can arbitrarily limit speech in this way, then there is no principle of free speech left in America.

Before going any further let me say there certainly is speech that one "ought" not say at times or anytime. However, the "ought" not say is a question of proper behavior, morality, respect for others, courtesy, and basic love for your fellowman. It is the path of virtue, in other words. They ought not say is not an area for the law. We either have the principle of free speech or we do not. The principle either is or is not. There is no right not to be offended, and the very notion is in diametrical opposition to free speech. That fact alone, should be a clear indicator of its aim. This is simply a decoy or straw man in the assault on the principle and human right of free speech. Therefore, the attacks on specific examples of speech must be seen for what they are: An attack on the principle of free speech itself.

> Whereas if all stand upon one footing, being equally protected by law, as citizens, (not as saints), and one prevails over another by cool investigation and fair argument, then truth gains honor; and men more firmly believe it, than if it was made an essential article of salvation by law. Truth disdains the aid of law for its defense - it will stand upon its own merit. The heathen worshipped a goddess, called truth, stark naked, and all human decorations of truth, serve only to destroy her virgin beauty. It is error, and error alone, that needs human support; whenever men fly to the law or sword to protect their system of religion, and force it upon others, it is evident that they have something in their system that will not bear the light, and stand upon the basis of truth.
>
> John Leland 1754-1841, Native New Englander
> and Baptist Minister[13]

The method of cultural Marxism and the long march through western culture to destroy it still exists in almost all aspects of our culture. Recognition, awareness, and understanding of what is happening can be the first step in thwarting and defeating this destructive insanity. Something that is very helpful to me is to consider the apparent vice or virtue of the actors in this play. If a political or other leader is appealing to the vices of man such as envy, jealousy, disrespectful attitude, anger, bitterness, divisiveness, to aid in the advancement of his cause, then he is likely leading you down a bad path. Anytime anyone employs or suggests implicitly or explicitly the use of the lower nature of man, in other words vices such at jealousy, envy, division, strife, etc. to gain your favor, you should beware. This ought to be a red flag. Men of goodwill will not encourage you in this way. And if we feed our better human tendencies towards human virtue, we will all be less likely to fall into the bitter tar pit of vice. The same is true of the followers. My observation of the political correctness politicians and other advocates is that I see little or no respect for others, people are shouted down rather than listened to and conversed with. This is the long march of cultural Marxism on display.

Anthony Gramsci, founder of Italian Communism and author of *Prison Notebooks* wrote, "Socialism is precisely the religion that must overwhelm Christianity… In the new order, socialism will triumph by first capturing the culture via infiltration of schools, universities, churches and the media by transforming the consciousness of society."

The Vatican reported Gramsci had a deathbed conversion to Catholicism. This conversion of Gramsci, in my view, is a complete repudiation of his life as a hater of Christianity and advocate of socialism and communism. Some report that upon his deathbed he asked to kiss a small ceramic likeness of the baby Jesus shortly before he died.

Regarding the politicians and federal governments role in this movement, they are playing a large part. Washington is contributing to the division of this nation by the breaching of its constitutionally defined role. Washington is choosing sides in matters of conscience and, via political correctness, forcing the government or state opinion upon the rest of the country. This has the effect of pleasing some while angering others thereby dividing the people. This is forward to the past actions, of all those tyrant kings, queens and Prohibition Progressives. This is spilling over into everyday lives of Americans spreading further division in our society. Thus Washington D.C. is actively ruling and dividing the nation in many areas. Americans are frustrated for being ruled over by Washington. This has the effect of creating an overreaction where everyone just wants to have *their* king elected. Each is seeking to have political relief by having their *king* in office. We must resist this temptation, because it is selfish and will result in the same situation we have now with the roles or people reversed. You would simply be changing chairs with the tyrant or in other words replacing their king for yours, a rebound reaction to an overbearing government. There are no kings in America and the government is to be our servant not our master. What we need is just and equal application of the law and respect of our individual rights by upholding the Constitution. We also need a return to virtue within ourselves. Don't point to anyone, just impose a standard of virtue upon yourself and do your best from there. We respect ourselves best by respecting others. To me it's not about making America

> *There are no kings in America and the government is to be our servant not our master.*

great again, it's about making America, America again. If we seek and do that, she will be great again.

I listed a small amount of the bloody history of man earlier in this discussion for a reason. Do you know what that reason is? The reason is that, the right to conscience, in concept and in law, was given to each of us by the blood of all those people, and countless others, you read about earlier. Most all of those people lost their heads or were burned alive simply because they wanted to live according to their own conscious. Freedom, through the Pilgrims, escaped the jaws of tyranny and has been given as a gift to all Americans. You know what offends me? Not the man who speaks his mind, you at least know where he stands. No, it's the man that stands in the same blood pool as all those bloody tyrants, past and present, that seeks to deny the right of conscience to all but himself. He offends me!

The government that seizes the authority to deny one man's conscience, may soon get around to you.

The government that seizes the authority to deny one man's conscience, may soon get around to you. Never use the sword of the law against your neighbor's conscience.

> Let every man speak freely without fear, maintain the principles that he believes, worship according to his own faith, either one God, three Gods, no God, or twenty Gods; and let government protect him in so doing, i.e., see that he meets with no personal abuse, or loss of property, for his religious opinions. Instead of discouraging him with proscriptions, fines, confiscation or death let him be encouraged, as a

> free man, to bring forth his arguments and maintain his points with all boldness; then, if his doctrine is false, it will be confuted, and if it is true, (though ever so novel), let others credit it.
>
> John Leland 1754-1841, Native New Englander and Baptist Minister[14]

In many ways the right of conscience is very broad. This is true because a man's beliefs encompass much about his life and the decisions that follow throughout daily living. Conscience for the individual exists beyond speech and belief and involves a myriad of decisions that one makes during the course of living life. In principle, however, it becomes clearer to comprehend.

You have the natural moral right to your beliefs and the right to live and speak your beliefs anywhere you go without interference from anyone. All having the same equal right of conscience no one can infringe upon the other. For example, a recent President's Administration attempted to force its opinion of right of conscience in the bathroom gender issue. The Federal Government tried to force by law its opinion or belief (conscience) that a transgender person has the right to use the bathroom that corresponds to the sex the person identifies with. Let's stipulate to that for the moment. However, the 10-year-old boy or girl and others, for example, also have the right to have their privacy protected. Washington D.C. is choosing sides in a matter of conscience which it is forbidden to do by law in our Constitution. Our government is, at times, acting like a king or dictator and it will be neither in this country. This is the thing I spoke of earlier when I wrote about Washington D.C.'s overreach in matters of conscience. Nevertheless, the answer to the problem will be found by respecting each individual's right of privacy and conscience.

The dictatorial action that politically correct advocating politicians at times attempt, injures the rights of some while favoring the rights of others. This is exactly why universal, absolute moral law matters. We either have universal moral law that applies equally to all or we have arbitrary laws with no standard or basis, therefore no just authority in our government. You cannot force an individual to participate in something they find morally objectionable. You do not force a gay person, for example, against his right to live the lifestyle he chooses. Nor do you force a straight Christian baker to bake a wedding cake for a gay wedding if the Christian baker finds it morally objectionable to do so. You may not agree in either case, but again, all individual rights must be respected or there is no concept of individual right of conscience. And that would mean the death of freedom. All individual rights are not respected under the arbitrary, subjective, ever-changing, man-made moral code of political correctness. The fallacy of political correctness (cultural Marxism) in contrast to the wisdom of our Constitution, should be very clear by the bathroom gender, and other P.C. issues. If you will research the Frankfurt

Those who seek to use the power of law to force any man against his conscience are no part of the spirit of liberty.

School and cultural Marxism I think you will even more clearly see what is going on here. The constitutional solution must protect the liberty of all, not just a politically favored few. No man should be forced to act against his conscience. Those who seek to use the power of law to force any man against his conscience are no part of the spirit of liberty.

What we are witnessing here is the assault on absolute universal moral law by an arbitrary, subjective, man-made moral system, namely political correctness or Cultural Marxism. You cannot remove mathematics from its universal absolute principles and still claim to have mathematics. You cannot remove moral value judgments from its universal absolute standard found in natural law because you then have no standard with which to make any value judgment at all. At this point the whole thing will collapse. You will then have a government that can act upon its own arbitrary, subjective, and morally relative authority, just like the kings of old. What is really happening here is an attempt to: 1. bring about the subversion of natural law, which would, 2. relegate our constitution moot or irrelevant, and 3. give our government authority over our individual right of conscience.

Just as in the area of speech, the same tactic is being used here. Our rights are being assaulted on the level of principle, but by the stealth method of a single-issue attack. It is the one slice at a time approach to taking the whole pie. Make no mistake about it, what the progressive movement is really after, is denying the right of conscience, just like the kings of old. Past politically correct advocating administrations have gone after this issue numerous times already. Catholic nuns, for example, were recently in front of the Supreme Court defending their right of conscience to object to birth control use, due to one such administration.

Division of opinion can be very healthy, but division of principle will cause the death of our nation.

Division of opinion can be very healthy, but division of principle will cause the death of our nation. Having the freedom to enjoy the rigorous debate of varying opinions without threat was given to us by the blood of our forefathers in the New World and Old. By Washington, D.C., taking it upon itself to choose societies winners and losers and backing that choice with the force of law, we are being divided on matters of opinion in matters of conscience. To be clearer, Washington is choosing sides in a matter of conscience, which it has no authority to do, and placing the force of law behind the choice thereby infringing upon the rights of others. One group, therefore, becomes the victor of arbitrary authoritarian government rule and the other group in society becomes the loser, thus becoming upset or angry. This is un-American and this was never the design nor the cause of America. Because Washington is using the force of law behind matters of conscience the public is becoming angry with one another and divided. We are being played, or better said, divided against ourselves. Washington is manipulating our healthy division of opinion by choosing sides in order to create a deadly division of principle.

It is time to wake up. This is not a game to the authoritarian personality, these people play for keeps. The brief account of the small bit of history that was mentioned earlier should make that clear. We should enjoy our lives, but mind its responsibilities as well. Vigilance to guard freedom for all is one of those responsibilities. Love your neighbor as yourself, and do not force any man against his own conscience. Take a stand for all individuals right of conscience not just those you happen to agree with. Never participate in the tyranny over another man's conscience. To do so places you in the same blood pool of all the tyrants past and present.

The real crux of the matter, in my view, is this. There is a war being waged, against our culture which is based upon moral absolutism with its equal individual human rights under natural moral law, by subjectivism of a powerful arbitrarily-ruled state (political correctness and cultural Marxism). The prize for political correctness is the destruction and the control of the west with America being the crown jewel. The historical fact of the Christian principles of America's founding aided greatly in the propelling of her rise to power. It also created the largest middle class known to the world and helped to spread the cause of freedom and improved standards of living here and abroad. All of this as the consequent of America's founding principles. But the most important thing of all about the founding of America is this: America's patriots gave life to the miracle that was the greatest single power shift in the history of mankind. You know what that was? America and her patriots fought through the blood of tyranny for the self-evident sovereign rights of man—and won!

America wrestled the head of humanity from under the chopping block of tyranny. America, for the first time in human history, placed government as the footstool and servant of the people. Consider for a moment the profundity of that great gift of love through the selfless shedding of the blood of our ancestors for the cause of freedom for us. No greater love hath a man than to lay down his life for his friend. America rebelled from tyranny, America shed her blood as did others in the Old World for the right to simply live as they believed. To simply live as one believes is such a serious threat to the authoritarian that he will rather chop off your head than simply grant your wish of freedom. Does this not tell you the price these personality types will pay to maintain authority over you?

America is the great land where we are free to be divided upon our opinions as long as we are united upon our principles of freedom.

Wake up America, wake up! Breathe new life in the true cause of America. Base your actions upon the cause of love of fellowman not down in the pit of bitterness, envy, fairness, and politics of division. America is the great land where we are free to be divided upon our opinions as long as we are united on our principles of freedom. The politically correct and social justice advocating politicians and citizens, whether intentional or not, are attempting to destroy our principles by manipulating the division of our opinions. There is no spoken division of opinion where tyrants reign. Run from those men who espouse such false teaching.

Thomas Paine wrote in *Common Sense* in 1776, "The cause of America is in a great measure the cause of all mankind."

The Takeaway for Freedom's Defense: Defending the individual right of conscience for each of us defends freedom for all of us. Freedom of conscience must stand no matter the cost or our freedom will be lost.

Chapter 3

The Moral Law of Nature

The Assault on Freedom: Nature's moral law is under attack by cunning men who seek authority over man. Their scheme to undermine natural law and obtain this authority: The implementation of the arbitrary rules of social justice and political correctness.

> "The state of nature has a law of nature to govern it, which obliges everyone and reason, which is that law, teaches all mankind, who will but consult it, that being all equal and independent, no one ought to harm another in his life, health, liberty, or possessions......"
>
> John Locke
> Two Treatises of Government 1689 [15]

> "We hold these truths to be self-evident.."
>
> Declaration of Independence, July 4, 1776

Natural Moral Law (Laws of Nature) is the innate, eternal, and universal moral code which enables man to know right and wrong, good and evil, etc. Our country is founded upon the rational order which nature's moral law provides. The natural authority of the moral law is therefore above man and not in his direct control. This is not a "God debate," nor is it a debate or discussion of the "origin" of nature's universal, absolute, and fixed moral law. So often it seems that any discussion of morality presupposes a discussion of religion or God. Not at all. This is, however, a discussion of the real, immutable, absolute, fixed and eternal nature of the laws of nature. Specifically, this is a discussion of the particular area of natural law which establishes the laws of human behavior or conduct. In other words, morality. Why? Because its absolute, universal, fixed or unalterable discoverable truth is the very foundation of our constitution and country.

If nature's moral and science laws were random and undiscoverable, man could make little or no use of them. The natural laws of morality and science being precise, predictable, discoverable, repeatable, and absolute or fixed in nature are governed by nature's laws and principles to make it useful to man. In this way by discovering and utilizing the natural laws of nature, man is able to bring order to his existence, is able to invent useful tools, and construct a just constitutional government, by the consent of the governed. If our world were not governed by absolute immutable moral or scientific laws, we would have no hope of any possible order or advancement of our existence in matters of science or civil society. Specifically, for this discussion, the focus is on the natural moral law, as civil society would be unachievable absent an immutable absolute moral standard with which man is able to make clear value judgments and therefore just laws. Absent these standards of natural moral law, any attempt of man at government would be arbitrary, chaotic, subjective, and, therefore, forever unjust to all concerned. It would truly be the rule of the jungle.

Two possibilities exist for there to be an absence of this moral standard. First, for the standard not to exist in the first place, but the self-evident and universal nature of the moral law stands as a bulwark against this argument. Some seek this path anyway. Who knows why, especially in light of the self-evident nature of natural moral law. Self-evident natural moral guideposts such as the difference between honesty and dishonesty, purchasing something versus stealing something, sexual consent between a couple and rape, etc. These are examples of the self-evident moral law of nature. Perhaps it is natural for man to rebel against a standard of behavior he did not institute. Second, that man chooses to simply ignore or alter the moral law in favor of other arbitrary man-made or man-contrived standards such as moral relativity, and the implementation of moral relativity through the arbitrary schemes of social justice, and political correctness, etc. The first is natural, self-evident, universal, and so obviously not man-made or contrived. Thus it is called natural law, and the beauty is that not having made it, man is not in control of its existence and therefore man cannot alter or remove it. Natural law is there whether we like it or not. It is there whether we ignore it or not. Natural moral law is immutable. Natural moral law is truly a just and independent standard for all. It exists independent of opinion and argument to the contrary.

The second, moral relativity, being arbitrary has to be explained to those who would be supposed to live under its magistrate. The obvious arbitrary nature of morality being relative is clear from the start as evidenced by its name, moral relativity. Therefore, any hope of utilizing it as a system of justice for society is completely farcical at the outset. This seems self-evident, does it not? Lastly, and most heinous, it places man in charge of the relative moral standard rather than the objective absolute standards of the natural laws of nature. This is perhaps the most damning reason of all for any such attempt at man-made moral judgments or systems. The bias of man under any morally relative system should be obvious to any reasonable and thinking person, in my view. This brings us back to the only possible standard, and that is the moral law of nature.

Thus, these natural laws of science and moral behavior form the foundation and possibility for civil society to exist. The degree of civility within society depends, then, upon the degree to which its citizens understand, agree, abide by, and live the natural moral law. Thus it behooves society to promote the standards of natural moral law for its own good and for the preservation of it for posterity.

Every child that is born has a consistent universal and ubiquitous thread of natural moral law within his or her conscience. When a child responds with "that is mine," "you promised," "I was here first," and so on, the child is making value judgments based on an innately understood and universal moral standard. This is self-evident *evidence* of the existence of natural moral law. Morality is that self-regulating guiding force which aids individuals and societies in positively assisting literally billions of human interactions on a daily basis. Imagine life without this universal and natural guidance system possessed by each of us. No amount of laws or government regulation can replace the positive and peace contributing effects of morality or, in other words, the moral law.

Morality is the greatest peace keeping force known to man.

Morality is the greatest peace keeping force known to man. Moreover, natural law has also given us a private and personal obligation to ourselves, our Maker, and a public civic obligation to our fellowman. The former being one's personal beliefs or ideas of God, lifestyle choices, etc. The latter being our obligation to peacefully live with our fellowman in order to promote civil society. It is critical to understand that one can have the former at variance with his neighbor without negatively impacting the latter. Thus, the Christian and atheist, gay or straight, for example, can easily be friendly neighbors by adhering to natural moral law and simply showing respect for one another and his natural rights. Natural moral law, when honestly utilized, places every man on an equal, constitutional, legal, and moral footing and one person is not subjugated or placed into submission to the other. That would be against natural law or in other words, immoral.

The Founder's Bible[16] "...for as a matter of civil policy it matters not one wit if my neighbor is an atheist or opponent of Christianity, but if he will nevertheless govern his behavior by the basic values found in the Ten Commandments - That is, if he will refrain from killing me, stealing my property, or taking my wife - he will make a good citizen, regardless of whether or not he holds any specific religious belief."

Just as in the area of moral behavior, there exists a private or personal duty or obligation to do one's best and a civic or public responsibility to do likewise. All men have free moral agency or license, thus, one's private affairs are between the individual and his Maker, if he so happens to believe in any Maker. Our civic responsibility to one another is something we all have a stake in and, therefore, a say in the matter. For example, if a person or group seeks to undermine or fundamentally transform the natural moral laws that all men have unalienable individual rights held individually by each man, I will then stand against that man in reason and principle.

> "As usurpation is the exercise of power, which another hath a right to, so tyranny is the exercise of power beyond right, which nobody can have a right to. And this is making use of power anyone has in his hands, not for the good of those under it, but for his own private separate advantage," says John Locke in Two Treatises of Government (1689, Sec. 199) [17]

As we have discussed, natural law places man equal to man, with no one being subjugated to the other. With no man having authority over another man. Just government is by equal consent only. Unfortunately, the right of man to live free and to exercise his unalienable rights is simply at odds with some men's views. The unfortunate reality is that some people in their private lives as well as the public arena simply seem to seek power over others. They seem to express a "know better" attitude. This attitude is of little consequence if it stopped there. However, these personality types will, as history proves, seek to arrange whatever necessary to ascend to power over others. Deception being chief among their tools of choice.

"The price of freedom is eternal vigilance" (Thomas Jefferson).

Thus: "The price of freedom is eternal vigilance" (Thomas Jefferson).[18]

History is replete with kings, queens, dictators, and tyrants. In other words, statists or progressive big government bureaucrats who believe that man's rights are not from natural law, but are determined by the state or government. This shift of derivation of rights from nature and nature's God (per U.S. Constitution and Declaration of Independence) to the state (which is man) must not be missed. This is huge. So huge, in fact, that this shift, if successful, would fundamentally transform or undermine the entire founding principles of our country. This attempt to subvert your individual ownership of your natural God given rights places the control of those rights back to the state. This would, in effect, nullify the American Revolution and our Constitution. Your individual *human rights* come from nature and nature's God. Therefore, no person, entity, government, kingdom, or whatever, exists between you and those rights. You must fully grasp this point. Your human rights are unalienable. They are a part of your existence just as is your body, your mind, and spirit. They are yours individually. In certain matters you answer to yourself and God alone (if you believe in God). You are entirely free to make that choice and to pursue your happiness based upon that choice and all it entails provided, in so doing, you do not trample another's right to the same. The statist/progressive big government bureaucrat seeks to replace the laws of nature with the authority of the state. The effect of that places man over the control of the state and initiates the loss of your human rights. Rights then become arbitrary in accordance with whoever is in charge of the state at the time. A few statist authoritarians of the past and present are Hitler, Stalin, Kim Jong Un, Fidel Castro, and his brother Raúl.

The statist seeks to socially engineer society to his vision of social justice or moral relativity, placing himself as arbiter-in-chief.

Never allow the statist to come between you and your natural human rights. This is what Thomas Jefferson was talking about when he spoke of being eternally vigilant. The statists attack natural law because it forbids them from having arbitrary control over what is right and wrong and other value judgments within our society. The statist seeks to socially engineer society to his vision of social justice or moral relativity, placing himself as arbiter-in-chief. Statists or progressives attack natural moral law by subtle and nefarious methods.

Some of the methods statists use to do this are:

- Executing emotionally solicitous and cunning arguments.
- Employing deceit
- Encouraging men toward exercising their vices against one another
- Being generally divisive
- Pointing out differences among men and claiming one to be the victim of the other
- Declaring these differences to be an injustice, ignoring the many natural reasons as well as government caused reasons for these differences.

Abhorrent encouragement of men to appeal to their lower nature engenders growth of jealousy, envy, and strife and division among our society members. This implements a form of Plato's *Noble Lie*, that this is the path to a better place for them in society. When men feel abandoned or left out of society and turn away from their moral senses under duress, economic, or otherwise, this method is appealing. Quite a convenient state of affairs, by the way, for the statist after more than 100 years of progressive statist big government. Statists have led America into regulatory bondage and massive debt—the progressive's gift to posterity.

Men who maintain their moral bearings are much less likely to follow statists who suggest the way to a better life is through the feeding of one's lower impulses. Self-maintenance of our moral bearings helps make us less inclined to be jealous and bitter of the differences between our fellowmen. My hope is that we will once again recognize that the tree of vice will not bring forth the fruits of virtue. Never follow someone who attempts to encourage the feeding of your vice rather than your virtue. This man is an imposter to virtue and will not have your interest in mind, only his. This will only empower the statist by pitting one citizen against the opinion and under the financial thumb of the other. This is the road to serfdom.

The tree of vice will not bring forth the fruits of virtue.

> "The Statist cannot abide the existence of natural law and man's discovery of 'unalienable' rights bestowed on all individuals by their Creator" (Mark R. Levin, *Liberty and Tyranny*, p. 29).[19]

A man who divides is attempting to conquer. The statist or progressive seeks to replace or corrupt natural moral law with his arbitrary notions of moral relativity and other man-made moral schemes such as social justice and political correctness. Sadly, it seems, too many fail to realize this shifts power from the individual to the state. This happens because schemes such as social justice, with names sounding worthy of their causes, appeal emotionally to many of us because we all prefer justice over injustice and what is correct over what is incorrect. The problem is that any system other than natural law is an arbitrary invention of man and is therefore by nature unjust. This is true no matter how well sounding the name may be. Most importantly, it is a shifting of power from the individual and his rights under universal natural law to the state as the subjective arbiter of what is socially just.

A question. Who wields more power on the field, that great athlete of your favorite sport *or* the referee who holds the rule book and the power to enforce the rules? Social justice removes universal natural law as the standard of all our rights and hands that "rule book of rights" back over to the subjective and arbitrary power of the state. Social justice, like political correctness, is an immoral and unjust scheme which assaults the natural moral law. Within it are the seeds of societal decline and destruction which will increase the power of the state by necessity. This is by design. Social justice is a direct cannon blow to the ship of liberty. Social justice is an assault against natural moral law in an attempt to fundamentally transform the basis of our constitutional government. The American Revolution was fought over the notion of mankind being free under nature and nature's law as opposed to

Social justice is an assault against natural moral law in an attempt to fundamentally transform the basis of our constitutional government.

mankind being under the control of the state as king. The result of America and its revolution was the removal of man—at least in America—from under the authority and control of the state. Statists have been seeking to reverse this ever since. Hence, if we are to remain free we must pay to toll of being forever vigilant.

Three men ran a foot race of a certain distance. Man A finished first, Man B finished second, and Man C finished third. Subsequent races show similar results. Each man desired to finish first. Each man did his best. Each man congratulates the other for a good performance by all. Natural law reveals itself here as each man, though perhaps not pleased with his performance, accepts the results as being the natural consequence and representation of the different abilities of the participants on that day. Everyone is fine with the results as each was free to do his best. It was a great race and all, including the onlookers, are quite content with the results of the competition. As part of natural law, mankind is innately predisposed to accept such outcomes as fair and just. Was there disappointment for some? Of course, and this will perhaps be a goad to increase the efforts and competition the next time.

Now consider this, as you recall the story. Does any man have a natural sense of being wronged? No! Why? Because each knows it was a fair and just race. Let's call this the natural order of fairness. Because of man's innate ability to naturally synthesize and make moral judgments about the race and all its interactions, in much the same way, a large crowd of strangers, perhaps a few friends as well, all enjoyed the same race. All made the same or very similar moral value assessments of the race and there was no bickering concerning the fairness or justice of the event. The common response to a commonly viewed event is the miracle of natural moral law. When it is willingly obeyed by individual free will, civil order is the result. Order which moral law of nature has everything to do with, and government has little or nothing to do with. Men who will not govern themselves are doomed to be ruled by others. Absorb that for a moment. Without natural law, general agreement of common value judgments among men would be all but impossible. Therefore, when someone seeks to replace this natural system within all of us with an alternate arbitrary system, red flags should fly. The moral law is based upon laws of nature just as is physics, mathematics, biology, etc. We cannot alter or ignore it without severe negative consequences any more than we can alter the natural laws of mathematics. The laws of nature exist independent of man. We can ignore them. We can pretend they are not there. However, truth exists independent of opinion. Man can choose to ignore the natural law but he cannot choose to ignore its consequences. We can choose to discover and utilize it for the benefit of man, or we can play pretend and experience the increased human suffering sure to follow.

Men that will not govern themselves are doomed to be ruled by others.

Hold on. A man from the government office of social justice has just arrived and called everyone back to the arena. This person is insisting that the race was not fair at all. Now murmurings are beginning to be heard throughout the crowd. He insists all race participants be awarded the same result—a *participation* award, he calls it. He claims, as he explains to the crowd, the competition is unfair and unjust because some are naturally faster than others so the game is naturally rigged. He maintains Man C will always finish last under natural law so the results must be equalized. Moreover, he says the self esteem of Man C has now been damaged and Man A has become arrogant due to winning. He hands out a paper to all participants congratulating them for their participation but no winner awards are allowed under social justice due to the prior stated reasons. The social justice official is proud of himself for masterminding a result of managed or forced equality of outcome. He calls this government-controlled outcome *social justice*. Now the crowd is arguing and yelling loudly at one another because they are all keenly aware of the social injustice that has occurred. Even the race participants themselves are arguing. The whole place is in an uproar. Arguments ensue about the nature of fairness and justice. The whole thing is now a contrived mess due to the intervention of the notion of social justice and its attempt to create an alternate moral code. There is no justice now, no fairness, and the anger from the crowd is almost palpable. It is a complete manipulated mess where no one any longer understands the rules of conduct. It is now a tower of Babel of moral relativity, where confusion and chaos reign.

We have a natural and discoverable system of order that exists independent of man, and for good reason. Man cannot change the laws of nature. He can only pretend he can, and at his own detriment. I accept natural law as it is self-evident. I know I am not God, and I must live under rules of natural law that I did not make. My opinion is that some men are simply discontent with this reality and they rebel against it, which is one's right for many reasons. A good topic for another day.

The pursuit of equality is a morally blind sprint to bondage. Equality is not a natural state. Equality exists nowhere in nature. I conclude from my observation of nature, then, that equality is not something that nature desires. The driving force of nature, once set in motion by the Creator (there is no requirement to agree on a Creator), is to survive. Thus, nature is always in survival mode. Therefore, if equality was of importance to survival would nature surely not provide humanity with at least one example? Just one? It is self-evident that nature likes similarity within a species but it does not produce exact sameness within any species. The state of equality would be the weakest of all possible constructs within the state of nature. For if there was a disease or some natural flaw an entire species could easily be wiped out. Thus natural diversity of similarity within any particular species seems to be preferred by nature. This natural diversity (as contrasted to forced diversity or sameness) is nature's way of strengthening and ensuring the survival of a species. Seems to me a good model for man. Natural law—the gift that keeps on giving every time it's tried.

Equality, then, is an unnatural state. An unnatural state cannot exist absent external forces while a natural state certainly can. Take a bridge for example, or a building of any sort. The materials and labor making up the structure are not situated in a natural state. A state of nature for these building materials would be a pile of material randomly strewn about. The engineered or coerced state brings about a structure which is very useful to man and is a positive contribution to his existence. This man-made yet unnatural arrangement of material matter serves man very well. However, it is one thing when man desires to engineer the material world to his liking, but it is quite another when in one man's arrogance he assumes the rightful authority to coerce or engineer the lives of his fellow human beings. Human beings are not parts of a larger personal construct simply waiting to be placed in society by the social engineer. Human beings all deserve the right to place themselves within the society according to their efforts and natural desires. Anything less amounts to bondage of one man over another. Subjugation or human usury is immoral. Forcing men (legal coercion) into an unnatural state of some arbitrary notion of social justice is no justice at all. Mankind is born to be free. Free to be lazy, to be industrious, creative, poetic, inventive, studious, to believe in God or not, and on and on. Should the fattest frog at the pond demand of all the others to obey him as he insists, because he is fat enough to force his will on the others? Would that unnatural state be fair or would it simply be the arrogance of the fattest frog expressed through coercion?

The point here is that coerced equality, or even the pursuit of it, is an unnatural social state of affairs. Any unnatural social construct would require external forces acting upon it, by force, to keep the construct existing. Now, where does one suppose this force to come from? The statist or progressive government of course. The net result of forced societal constructs is a government that uses force to maintain it. Force will create unrest. Unrest will create need for more force and on and on it goes. The natural state of mankind is freedom. Yes, there will be natural differences but those differences will certainly be held to a natural minimum if the federal government will serve its constitutional role to protect our rights instead of intruding upon them and leave the rest to the states and the citizens. No amount of machinations the statist/progressive can conjure will be sufficient to maintain an unnatural social order.

Under the umbrella of protection of the self-evident God-given natural moral law all men are free.

Under the umbrella of protection of the self-evident God-given natural moral law all men are free. Here is what I call the paradoxical genius of America: it is under the Christian founding and notion of nature and nature's God that the American

Constitution was created to protect the rights of *all* men. This Christian concept of our founding under natural rights protects the atheist, pagan, agnostic, homosexual, Christian, etc. Alexis de Tocqueville wrote in *Democracy in America*, 1835, "Christianity, which has declared that all men are equal in the sight of God, will not refuse to acknowledge that all citizens are equal in the eye of the law."[20]

No man who respects the natural rights of man should be feared. The Christian has no need to fear the atheist and vise versa. The gay, the straight and on and on, as long as we live under natural law and nature's God and not under man. So often I hear someone say they fear a Christian in politics because he may force him or her to do thus and so. A Christian may say the same of an atheist politician and so on. The statist or progressive has spread this fear. You will recall it is the statist or progressive who seeks to replace natural law with his own arbitrary moral code. This is what you should fear and that should be clear by this point. The statist or progressive does not believe in natural law and individual rights. The statist believes in the state's right to compel behavior according to its own arbitrary code. That is bondage, not freedom. Choose freedom. An easy way to detect a statist or progressive is that their solutions always seek more government authority and usually take away a part of your rights and freedom for the promise of your security and the greater good of society. Apply this test to assess the governmental landscape. You may be amazed at the results of the names that will likely surface from all political parties. Statists/progressives are found in them all. It is only the constitutionalist that will seek to keep the government off your individual rights.

One final note on this issue and the paradoxical genius of America. I have for many years been puzzled by the arguments over church and state in America. The statists and progressives have used this argument, to the extent possible, to exclude the influence of Christianity from public institutions, etc. A very deceptive about face of America's founding. The statist seeks power to implement a forced, unnatural, and unprincipled arbitrary moral code of social justice by denying justice (respecting the rights of all) of some members in society, in order to force a supposed state of equality of outcome on others. He then calls it *social justice*. Moreover, with all too much success, the statist's cry is that the religious man (Christian namely), must be watched carefully so as not to force his way on the lot of us. If allowed, he claims, the Christian will merge church and state thereby endangering our whole system. The inference being the Christian is to be feared, in government especially. The statist makes this claim against and aimed primarily toward the very group of religious people who gave our country the concept of individual rights, and that government's primary role is the protection of these rights. The statist or progressive seeks to merge his religion of secular humanism and materialism (belief that nothing exists beyond the material world) with the state and thereby undermine natural law in favor of social justice and political correctness. For what is religion if not a system or code of belief, and there are many. To those who claim no religious belief whatever, you prove my point. Political zealots come in many forms.

> "Neither the wisest constitution nor the wisest laws will secure the liberty and happiness of a people whose manners are universally corrupt" Samuel Adams[21]

The Takeaway for Freedom's Defense: To understand what natural law is, is to understand that it is the foundation of your freedom— a natural morality grounded in reason, coming from nature, eternal, innate to the mind of man, and fundamental to our freedom, peace, and happiness in the civil society.

Chapter 4

Know the Principles of Freedom

The Assault on Freedom: America's true history, the emancipation of man from government, is not taught as it once was. This is a passive aggressive assault, which, by omission of teaching, erodes and destroys the source of her greatness, the principles of God-given individual freedom.

> "Those who expect to reap the blessings of freedom, must, like men, undergo the fatigues of supporting it."
>
> Thomas Paine[22]
>
> "Eternal vigilance by the people is the price of liberty, and that you must pay the price if you wish to secure the blessing."
>
> Andrew Jackson[23]

We all have a responsibility to be informed. A responsibility to yourself, to the ones you love, and to the ones to come after you. Imagine that a son has been given a new car by his parents. Only a few short months later he managed to scrape the side of it against a tree, forgot to put the parking brake on and let it roll into a neighbor's car, ran too long with a flat tire increasing the repair expense by ruining the rim, and never having checked the oil. To add insult to injury he has gotten several speeding violations thereby increasing the insurance cost. And lastly, he has not even bothered to keep it clean. He has simply abused and trashed it. A tragic situation to be sure, but the tragedy is not only about the car itself. The greater tragedy is in the lack of responsibility of the recipient, the young apparent ingrate who wants to call himself a man. It is one thing if the story stopped there, but suppose the parents told the child that the car was for his use during his college years and then it must be passed to his younger sister for her use during her college years. What a selfish person you are no doubt thinking. “Aw, it doesn’t matter," he says, "The thing still works.” Really? Does it? For how much longer? Now repairs must be made to fix the damage. And at whose expense will that be?

A race to the bottom may seem like careless fun ‘til you get there. I can probably guess what most of you thought about the hypothetical above. What an irresponsible kid, right? The problem is instead of a car that cost dollars to purchase, we have squandered much of our freedom which cost the blood of real people to purchase. To purchase from whom? The ever lurking tyrant, of course. Do you think, a bear, that you have once shoed away from you barn store of meat is forever gone? We have been so blessed by the grace of God and by the blood of our forefathers that is in the soil we tread, that we are in many ways sadly not too unlike the kid above. Now we need to get about the business of repairs so that there is still freedom to pass along to those who come after us.

Know this truth, there is an age-old and seemingly eternal battle between man and man. In other words, an eternal battle for control. A battle between the men who simply wish to live and let live in freedom, and men who seek to rule over and control man. The latter often claim they are doing this for our own good. America for the first time in human history defeated the self-appointed rulers of men and gave the greatest gift ever given to man, from man. Freedom's gift was given to and for each one of us by our American ancestors, and we have a responsibility to pass it on. This was one of the greatest triumphs of mankind over himself in all of human history. This took great moral integrity, will, courage, and love to extend the banner of freedom to each making no man king, and placing government at man's feet instead of over his head. Only God is over man's head and we each determine that decision by ourselves free from coercion of man or state.

Nevertheless, the battle will never end and thus eternal vigilance is the order of today, tomorrow, and the next. Like taking our rest, meals, and exercise, the duty of watchfulness is the small price we bear for freedom. If we refuse to pay freedom's small and bloodless price of vigilance, perhaps we are not deserving of its rewards, but more deserving of the bondage that is sure to come. It is already all too near.

> Tyranny, like hell, is not easily conquered; yet we have this consolation with us, that the harder the conflict, the more glorious the triumph. What we obtain to cheap, we esteem to lightly: it is dearness only that gives everything its value. Heaven knows how to put a proper price upon its goods; and it would be strange indeed if so celestial article as FREEDOM should not be highly rated.
>
> Thomas Paine, The Crisis 1776 [24]

If we do not quickly regain the knowledge and thankfulness of the price and responsibility of freedom, surely Heaven will soon present us with freedom's price tag, but it may be our children who pay the bill. God forbid that we are like the kid and the car and do that to our children and posterity. So what do we do? What does it mean to be informed? What do I have to know to be informed? You may think, I want to be informed, but I work, have a family, thus my time is limited. There is also a large contingent of those who will say, what can you or I do? We can't do anything about it so why waste time on it?

Let me take the last thought first. Suppose you are in a coffee house with friends. You are having good conversation, laughing, just a good ole time together. Moments later a man in a red shirt comes rushing in. He is a bit sweaty and his hurried fashion catches the attention of most everyone. Nevertheless, he quickly begins to settle and slowly makes his way to order a coffee. No big deal so everyone returns to their own matters and acquaintances. Now consider a slightly different version of that scene. Imagine the exact same situation and you are there with your friends. This time, however, there is a radio playing in the background and the broadcast is interrupted for an emergency announcement. The announcement states that "a man in a red shirt has just robbed a bank and shot two people. It is believed he is still in the area and is attempting to hide in plain view by entering one or more of the local shops." What do you think the reaction of those in the coffee shop would be now that they are more informed? Perhaps subdue the man and call the police? Just by being informed we can all act responsibly when the time arises. That is the answer to the "what can I do" question. You can do a lot if you are informed. But most days you are required to do nothing. You simply just go about the enjoyment of your life. I am not suggesting giving up your life and committing to a lifestyle you have no desire to commit to as a non-politician. I do not care for that either. What I am suggesting is being informed in the principles of freedom and having at least a basic understanding of how America came to be and why those principles get applied in our lives. One does not have to become a lover of politics in order to do this. But simply being informed will help keep freedom alive when the man in the red shirt comes in the room, so to speak. That is what you can do. This alone is huge if we would but do it. You get and stay informed, then you just go on about your life and the things you enjoy. I am not talking about a full time job here. Knowledge is power. And knowledge with active vigilance of the principles of freedom will help ensure your freedom and that of your children and their children.

This may come as a shock to you. I disdain politics, and I have no taste nor patience for the many lies, inconsistencies, and downright deceptive, dishonorable, and mostly self-serving behavior that too many of our elected officials engage in. But I sure care about other men who are making rules I must live by, so I pay attention. The federal government passes laws we must obey, for example, and then exempts themselves from the very same laws. We are, by our tacit acquiescence, allowing the throne of tyranny to be rebuilt. Having said that, I hate tyranny even more. This nation has been in the flood-tide of progressive, ever expanding regulatory red-tape for more than one hundred years now, since at least 1913. Due to progressivism and statists that desire big government, we are awash in debt, regulation, our money has been gutted and devalued, freedoms once enjoyed are now trampled, and others threatened. I am confident enough in the study that I have made of our predicament and the conclusions I draw on the basis of my study to state that I think we are on the cusp of some of the most serious times our nation has seen in its entire history. The very basis of our system built upon the individual's right to life, liberty, and pursuit of happiness is hanging by a precarious thread.

A fundamental transformation is being attempted, and we must rise to the occasion and thwart it, if not for us for our children and posterity. Almost every day I see serious assaults made upon the principle of the right to bear arms (2nd Amendment), the principle of free speech, the principle of right of conscience, the principle of the right to own private property, the principle of protection against unreasonable searches and seizures, etc. There is a current unconstitutional practice of asset forfeiture occurring where cash or similar assets are simply seized from citizens without due process. In some cases, the police departments have been able to divide the loot between themselves. Pretty good motivation to seize assets don't you think? Look it up. It is happening. Do your own research, please.

A couple of examples: In a USA.com story Ken Quran a convenience store owner in N.C. had $153,907.99 dollars seized. After a long battle, the government was found in the wrong and his money was finally returned. Money seized with no trial and no charges. The same story goes on to state the government took about $43 million in 618 other cases between 2007-2013.[25]

In a Forbes.com article, Randy Sowers, a Maryland Dairy Farmer had his entire bank account wiped out. All $62,936.04 was emptied from his account under "structuring" regulations.[26] Laws regulating the cash transactions of money less than $10,000 dollars. So it is now illegal to withdraw or deposit our own money from our own bank accounts in the manner we choose. The article continues, and Randy is quoted at a hearing decrying "they could throw my wife in jail for depositing cash in a bank?" The article does say that after a four-year-long battle Randy Sowers was made whole because the U.S. Justice Dept. decided to return the seized cash. The colonialist dealt with these types of warrantless asset seizures from King George III. So the founding fathers created the 4th amendment to the constitution. It is as follows.

Amendment IV

> The right of the people to be secure in their persons, houses, papers, and effects, against unreasonable searches and seizures, shall not be violated, and no Warrants shall issue, but upon probable cause, supported, by Oath or affirmation, and particularly, describing the place to be searched, and the persons or things to be seized.

Our principles of freedom are being assaulted and fundamentally transformed. These assaults often appear to be superficial to certain issues, and thus seemingly insignificant or innocuous, but, make no mistake about it, the assault is aimed at the deeper level of the principle of freedom involved in the governing of that issue. Our principles of freedom are being assaulted at their core or foundation. Often times the surface issue being debated clouds the true principle being assaulted. The transgender bathroom issue is not just about where people use the bathroom. You have to ask yourself, what is the governing principle behind separate bathrooms to begin with. It is about the principle of the right of conscience. That is the reason for separate men's and women's rooms in the first place. It is a matter of respect and decorum for the privacy and conscience of each one of us. Some don't care who is in the bathroom with them, and that is their right, but others do and that is their right. We are a country of individuals, not groups, which means every one of us is precious and we matter as does the conscience rights of each. Political correctness and social justice advocates have attempted to assault that right of conscience for some while favoring that right for others regarding this issue. This is an assault on the principle of individual right of conscience itself. A fundamental constitutional individual right which we all have a God-given right to. Therefore, instead of being used as pawns against each other we need to humble ourselves, love one another regardless of our differences, and stand in locked-armed position to defend the principles of freedom for all people. Principles cannot be divided, only trampled, abused, and ignored. And this has been the want of tyrants throughout history, until America, until now. God forbid we turn back the tide of history after what our forefathers have done for us. If we allow by apathy or ignorance the tyranny of the past to become the reality of the future, then may God help us and posterity forgive us. This generation could be the source of great disdain for generations to come if we fail to recognize the current state of our union, and the threats to our liberty that are so clearly obvious.

If we allow by apathy or ignorance the tyranny of the past to become the reality of the future, then may God help us and posterity forgive us.

Forget unanimity in opinion. It will never happen nor should it. Forget unanimity of religion for it will never happen. Forget unanimity of this opinion or unanimity of that opinion for it will never happen. But never forget the unanimity of freedom's principles from which we all securely stand as free men and women. Freedom is the ultimate diversity program because freedom is the right to be different. Diversity of thought, religion, speech, lifestyle, you name it. Political correctness is the government's use of force to deny that right all while waving the banner of tolerance, diversity, and fairness.

Statists are inconsistent because they do not base their claims upon principles. If you pay attention you will spot these inconsistencies. I just gave you one as an example, a good one that they use frequently: They claim tolerance and diversity while enforcing intolerance and uniformity of thought and behavior. Political correctness secures nothing but intolerance of anything not sanctioned by the politically correct state. This is what I meant when I stated that your freedom is not paramount over the statist's agenda. Political correctness is a good example of that as well. Political correctness relies on emotion and not reason. Political correctness is an attempt to replace the natural moral law with a man-made counterfeit moral code.

Political correctness is an attempt to replace the natural moral law with a man-made counterfeit moral code.

When it comes to freedom's principles, tyranny over one citizen is tyranny over all citizens.

We need to look beneath the surface to the governing founding principle, because that is what is being attacked in each of these cases. It is imperative to see beneath the bathroom issue to the governing principle of right of conscience. It is likewise imperative to see beneath the "false right" claim of not being "offended," to the governing principle of free speech. It is important to see beneath the false claim of group rights where Christian bakers, Aaron and Melissa Klein of Oregon, were charged and fined $135,000.00 by a judge for their not baking a wedding cake for a gay couple. The Kleins also lost their store.[27] Someone could say that is silly, just bake the wedding cake. Even if you think one person's matter or belief of his conscience is stupid, naive, silly, antiquated, or whatever, it is still his right of conscience and it must be respected just as yours must be respected.

To the Kleins, this wasn't just any cake. It was a wedding cake that effectively made them part of the wedding process which they, in their conscience, objected to. It was their right. You cannot keep secure your individual rights while ridiculing and denying the very same rights of another citizen. When it comes to freedom's principles, tyranny over one citizen is tyranny over all citizens. A government capable of trampling one man's rights, is capable of

A government capable of trampling one man's rights, is capable of trampling all men's rights.

trampling all men's rights. It's just a matter of time. Moreover, would any of us want to force someone to bake our wedding cake? What does this say of the prosecuting citizen trying to force another citizen to bake a cake. This is a clue to the subterfuge which is obfuscating the real story beneath the story. This was a direct assault against the Klein's right of conscience and this is the story line here, not the cake. Which is the attempt at a fundamental transformation of our country, just as political correctness and social justice advocates seek to do. What does it say of people who create division with political and legal force in order to accomplish their political desires? Ponder that. Do not follow such people, follow your conscience and seek virtue within yourself and the people we elect. What are we becoming? We must stop this incessant labeling the voice of individual differences of conscience with the pejorative suffix "phobe" just because one disagrees with another's belief or right of conscience. America was never about unanimity of opinion toward the state or other matters. There are communist nations for that role. We, Americans, all believe different things and we must be respectful of each other if we are to remain free. To follow the tyrant's lead down this road of division based upon varying and differing opinions will lead us to the destruction of our principles which are the foundation of the freedom upon which we all stand. If this happens we all go down.

To force a man by the sword of the law against his own conscience aligns one with the tyrants of the past and present. Do not stand with tyrants. If a man's belief in a matter, is truly ridiculous, why the need for ridicule? Just walk away and leave him be. We must not do this to one another. All men have a right to their beliefs and all men stand upon the very same principles that secure these rights. Is it not self-evident that to attack, ridicule, label, or deny one's right to his belief is to pound away at the foundation of freedom beneath your own feet of the very same principle you yourself are standing upon? The same principle you stand upon for your right to your belief to perhaps disagree with the baker? Our principles are under attack via seemingly innocuous, benign, or superficial issues like bathroom selection, gender pronouns, and wedding cakes. Always ask yourself—what is the governing principle beneath the surface issue. And that is a natural segue to the way I think one can best get informed and stay informed.

So what to do? Most of us find it quite difficult to get a good handle on political affairs for several reasons. First, it seems that to have any notion of what is going on in our government one must make a full time effort to the task. Who has time for that, or even less the desire? Even for those who do have time for that, there is little interest and patience to wade through all the media and political sophistry, you know, arguments that sound plausible on the surface but are filled with fallacy and political double speak. Yet it remains, that absent vigilance our greatest asset can become our greatest liability. We are free to choose apathy, but we must resist this and choose wisely. Therefore, we must be vigilant regarding our freedom. We have no real choice.

Nevertheless, there is still the issue of what to do because the wolf is always lurking. Hyperbole? A little over the top you say? The Fabian Socialist Society's symbol is a wolf in sheep's clothing. It can be seen in their infamous stained glass window designed by George Bernard Shaw. Matthew 7:15 says, "Be aware of false prophets, who come to you in sheep's clothing, but inwardly are ravenous wolves."

Howard Stern, "The wolves are always plotting..." Stern made this statement in a broadcast segment in support of the 2nd Amendment. For accuracy and clarification sake: Stern, to my knowledge, was only making the point criminals and terrorists are the wolves. However, the Fabian Socialist Society in its own symbolic proclamation states about itself that it is a wolf in sheep's clothing.

> *"I appeal to the chemists to discover a humane gas that will kill instantly and painlessly..."*
> *- George Bernard Shaw, Fabian Socialist & Playwright*

In a Youtube.com video, George Bernard Shaw (a Fabian Socialist) speaks about citizens coming before a death panel every so many years to justify their existence. If they can't, well they get euthanized, humanely, of course, says Shaw. "I appeal to the chemists to discover a humane gas that will kill instantly and painlessly..."[28] Freedom has enemies. Why? It seems counterintuitive doesn't it? I agree, until you understand there are those who place a higher premium upon their political agendas, and belief system, than your freedom.

All the kings, queens, dictators, tyrants, progressives, and statists of the past and present do this very thing. Man granting freedom to man by consent of the governed in America was a historic act of civic benevolence between fellowmen. Ponder that then compare and contrast that great act in American history to the acts of the statists, progressives, kings, queens, dictators and tyrants. These types seek to divide men against each other thereby securing the power of government for themselves. The more divided a populous the more the government is strengthened. The opposite is also true here in America. Again, the formation of American government was an act of benevolence that man granted freedom to one another. That is where we must return our hearts to.

The toils of earth do not exist in heaven so we have something to look forward to. But for now we all need to have some modicum of information to maintain freedom for our lives and pass it on for the next generation. It is our responsibility to do so, like it or not. If you understand the rules of baseball you can fully participate in the enjoyment and advancement of the game even if you have no clue to the names of the players, their personal lives, past or present. The same is true of our principles of freedom. Don't spend all your time chasing the names and goings on of the political characters. Look beneath the political soap opera and watch what they do regarding the principles of freedom. They will either support of undermine the principles of our constitutional freedom.

Endeavor to understand the rules of the game of freedom, so to speak. When a rule or principle is being broken or advocated to be broken, you will recognize this and you will know how to respond accordingly. To be informed of any sport, means to know its rules. Personal information of the players, coaches, etc. may be curious to some, but it is irrelevant to the game and application of the rules. In much the same way knowing the principles of freedom is what is required to maintain it. Knowledge of the personal goings on of the politicians should be of secondary importance and knowledge of the principles of freedom should be primary. Trying to become informed any other way is like chasing one's tail in an exercise of futility. This is especially true in our age of information overload, and downright lack of good solid "truth reporting."

The best way to help secure our remaining freedoms and regain lost freedoms is for all of us to understand the principles from which freedom comes. If you understand the principles that govern our system and guard our freedom, then it becomes a much easier task of staying informed and weeding out the charlatans that would deceive and charm your freedoms from your grasp. There are signs that indicate the proper direction in life if one knows how to read them. Understanding the governing principles of our country will help you in this effort. I am a constitutionalist and therefore believe in a small federal government as the constitution prescribes. I believe in limited government in which the government gets out of our private lives and leaves us alone. If you will read the constitution, and you should, you will see that the role of the federal government is very limited. For the past one hundred years or more it has usurped authority far beyond its constitutionally defined role and scope. You cannot know this if you do not read the document. Please read it and also read the Declaration of Independence. Once you have done this you will be well on your way to being an informed citizen.

Next, know what the Bill of Rights is and study it until you understand the governing principles behind each right. The Bill of Rights is the first 10 amendments to the Constitution. This is important to do because this is what is going to help you to identify the charlatans of freedom. The unprincipled man is no friend of freedom and you need to be able to spot them.

Freedom of speech is based upon the principle that every individual has a right to his own thoughts and the right to voice them without fear. This single principle governs the right of millions of people to hold millions of different opinions in peace—beautiful isn't it. Now, I bet you can easily see that political correctness is a clear and present threat to that principle and peace, right?

The Bill of Rights

Ratified December 15, 1791

Article I

Congress shall make no law respecting an establishment of religion, or prohibiting the free exercise thereof; or abridging the freedom of speech, or of the press; or the right of the people peaceably to assemble, and to petition the Government for a redress of grievances.

Article II

A well regulated Militia, being necessary to the security of a free State, the right of the people to keep and bear Arms, shall not be infringed.

Article III

No Soldier shall, in time of peace be quartered in any house, without the consent of the Owner, nor in time of war, but in a manner to be prescribed by law.

Article IV

The right of the people to be secure in their persons, houses, papers, and effects, against unreasonable searches and seizures, shall not be violated, and no Warrants shall issue, but upon probable cause, supported by Oath or affirmation, and particularly describing the place to be searched, and the persons or things to be seized.

Article V

No person shall be held to answer for a capital, or otherwise infamous crime, unless on a presentment or indictment of a Grand Jury, except in cases arising in the land or naval forces, or in the Militia, when in actual service in time of War or public danger; nor shall any person be subject for the same offence to be twice put in jeopardy of life or limb; nor shall be compelled in any criminal case to be a witness against himself, nor be deprived of life, liberty, or property, without due process of law; nor shall private property be taken for public use, without just compensation.

Article VI

In all criminal prosecutions, the accused shall enjoy the right to a speedy and public trial, by an impartial jury of the State and district wherein the crime shall have been committed, which district shall have been previously ascertained by law, and to be informed of the nature and cause of the accusation; to be confronted with the witnesses against him; to have compulsory process for obtaining witnesses in his favor, and to have the Assistance of Counsel for his defence.

Article VII

In Suits at common law, where the value in controversy shall exceed twenty dollars, the right of trial by jury shall be preserved, and no fact tried by a jury, shall be otherwise re-examined in any Court of the United States, than according to the rules of the common law.

Article VIII

Excessive bail shall not be required, nor excessive fines imposed, nor cruel and unusual punishments inflicted.

Article IX

The enumeration in the Constitution, of certain rights, shall not be construed to deny or disparage others retained by the people.

Article X

The powers not delegated to the United States by the Constitution, nor prohibited by it to the States, are reserved to the States respectively, or to the people.

Let's now look at the fourth amendment. "The right of the people to be secure in their persons, houses, papers, and effects, against unreasonable searches and seizures, shall not be violated…" So what is the governing principle here? The principle of the right to privacy. Now, knowing that the principle of right to privacy protects your privacy let me ask a question. A politician comes along and says that, for your protection and safety, we must capture all electronic data like e-mails, phone activity, texting, twitter, etc. Is this something you should go along with? No! Absolutely not because it is against your right of privacy. The

Benjamin Franklin said, "They who would give up an essential liberty for a little temporary security, deserve neither liberty or security."

government cannot constitutionally do this, but it does it anyway. Removing your rights will not keep you safe, it will make you less safe. Benjamin Franklin said, “They who would give up an essential liberty for a little temporary security, deserve neither liberty or security.”[29]

The NSA facility, National Security Agency, that gathers our electronic information is located in the state of Utah. Is this data capturing unconstitutional? Yes, you bet it is. What if I was capturing your data? Would you be outraged? You should be, not because you have anything to hide but because your right to privacy against unwarranted searches and seizures of your personal and private information is one of those precious principles of freedom. This constitutional breach is part of that loss of freedom I mentioned earlier. But at least, by knowing the principle involved you can more easily know when a politician is working for or against the constitution which in turn means you. Moreover, if a politician responds to a problem or crisis by desiring to remove your freedom, then you know he is a big government progressive—period. A constitutionalist will not attempt to resolve a national problem by removing or attacking your individual rights. He would rather strengthen them as to weaken them.

Every time there is a tragic shooting incident a progressive or statist always responds by attempting to attack your 2nd amendment rights to bear arms. Another big government progressive spotted. A man commits a crime, and the progressive statist wants to arrest the gun. A member of the British Parliament was shot to death in England. The irony? Guns are not available and illegal to own in England. The English have no second amendment rights. England is a gun-free zone as far as its citizens are concerned.

Switzerland, by contrast, requires each of its citizens to own a gun. You don't punish the law-abiding because of the crimes of the lawless. During the American Revolution a British general orders folio (official enemy notebook) was found by the Patriots. The folio contained the order that "His Excellency the commander-in-chief orders, that all inhabitants (American Patriots) who shall be found with arms, not having an officer with them, shall be immediately taken and hung-up." Had the American's obeyed the nonsense order there would be no America. So, what is the governing principle of the Second Amendment? You have the right to self defense. You are your first responder - The police investigate crimes, therefore, they are not in the role of your defense. They will investigate, however, after you have been shot because that is their role. They can't stop a crime that has not been committed, therefore your defense and safety is your responsibility.

A man commits a crime, and the progressive statist wants to arrest the gun.

You see how easy this gets once you understand the governing principles behind your rights. It will help you to see though the political fog that is blown in our faces every day. It will also help us respect our differences because our founding principles are the common ground that we all stand upon for the right to proclaim our differences. Principles are guideposts in practically all areas of our lives.

Let's now take a look at the tenth amendment. "The powers not delegated to the United States by the Constitution, nor prohibited by it to the states, are reserved to the states respectively, or to the people." What is the governing principle here? It is the governing principle of *limited federal government*. If you will look in the Constitution at Article I Section 8 you will see that there are 17 enumerated powers that the Federal Government has and all other matters "are reserved to the states respectively, or to the people." That is an exact quote from the 10th Amendment of the Constitution. In other words, all other matters are for the people—us. Yes, to you and me. We should be voting locally on so many issues that Washington, D.C., has nationalized. Yes, federalism not nationalism is the constitutional design of America. It is called federalism for a reason. Federalism grants certain rights (17 enumerated powers) to the federal government, while respecting the sovereignty of the states and you. Therefore, by knowing this governing principle, and by reading the 17 enumerated powers you see that the federal government is currently exercising powers beyond its constitutional authority.

For a primer I want to give you a few of the enumerated powers of the federal government. To coin money, to establish post offices, to punish counterfeiting, to borrow money on the U. S. credit. I wanted to include this because I want you to get the idea of these powers. Pretty boring and routine, right? Exactly, because the individual states are where all the action is supposed to be according to the Constitution, but we have allowed the opposite to occur. The federal government has no constitutional say in marriage, abortion, or who goes to which bathroom. It is not their business.

It is imperative to fully comprehend the concept and principle that when any branch of the federal government—supreme court, executive, or legislative branch—involves itself in particular matters of our private lives, such as abortion, marriage, bathrooms, etc. it is unconstitutionally nationalizing matters of your right of conscious. The federal government is then, in matters of individual choice and conscience, taking sides. This has the effect of dividing "We the people." This removes your freedom of individual choice.

The federal government is acting like a national government taking your freedom of choice or conscience away from you and your state. These matters, and others, are your business and the state in which you reside. That is the constitutional design of America that our forefathers shed their blood for. This must be corrected constitutionally and soon.

A question? What is the difference in a Washington D.C. that dictates by national fiat or decree all matters of conscience to us and a king, queen, dictator, tyrant, or progressive? None. The kingdom of D.C. is being constructed before our very eyes by attacking our founding principles and transferring our individual rights and sovereignty from We the people to the government.

James Madison, 4th President of the United States says in the Federalist Papers 39, “Each State, in ratifying the Constitution, is considered a sovereign body, independent of all others, and only to be bound by its own voluntary act. In this relation, then the new Constitution will, if established, be a federal, and not a national constitution.”[30]

Since you now know that the principle of limited federal government is what is supposed to govern the federal government, let me ask a question. What is the federal government doing involving itself in the abortion issue? What is the federal government doing involving itself into the healthcare issue? What about all the federal regulations that have citizens and businesses wrapped up like mummies?

I’ll tell you what they are doing. They are building a national leviathan which is undermining and assaulting our federalist system and, therefore, our freedoms and individual rights. Knowing the difference between federalism and nationalism is critical to understanding our American form of government and your individual rights and liberty. A national government is essentially a centralized system of government which governs an entire nation. A one size fits all philosophy to any and all issues. A federal government system, such as ours, is a limited federal government whereby the states and the citizens maintain their sovereignty independent from the federal government. The states established the federal government during the colonial era. The states are the parent, so to speak, of the federal government in constitutional America. The states created the federal government in Washington, D.C. and are therefore the true power centers of our nation. Because the federal government has usurped much of the authority of the states and weak states and governors have acquiesced to this unconstitutional federal governmental authority, this does not seem to be the case. Article V of the Constitution explains the role and power the states have to amend the constitution if necessary. The states are the final check on the federal government. Not the other way around as Washington, D.C would have us believe. The last thing the Founders would want after having defeated tyranny, would be to create a throne of centralized power for tyranny to begin all over again.

What is the governing principle behind someone's right to believe in whatever they choose to believe in? The right of conscience.

What is the governing principle behind the freedom of the press? The principle of the right of the people to be informed on the affairs of their government and nation.

I hope you are able to see what I am trying to convey here. If we will focus on the principles of freedom that govern our individual rights and our American system, it will be so much easier to know who to vote for and what side of an issue we think we should be supporting. Likewise, to not know and or understand these principles can easily have you landing on the wrong side of an issue. A warning: sadly, some people are just dishonest and deceptive, and they will use many emotional ploys and untruths to distract you from the governing principles of your freedom. Distractions like wedding cakes and bathrooms. Stay focused on the principles, maintain your reasoning abilities, and try not to get emotional. Emotion makes it easy for any of us to be led astray. That is why emotion is the weapon of choice of the demagogue. The rich man has his money to protect his rights but the common man needs the constitution. The constitution is the friend of the common man, and the enemy of the tyrant, progressive, or statist. That great document is most needed by the least among us. Let's breathe a new breath of life into it. We do this by understanding its principles and supporting all Americans' individual rights. Diversity of human individuality stands upon the foundation of unanimity of the principles of freedom. That's what is meant by "united we stand divided we

The rich man has his money to protect his rights but the common man needs the constitution.

Freedom once obtained, is not freedom forever secured!

fall." United on the principles of freedom, thus free to lead diverse lives of our own choosing.

Do you know how the founders came up with the Bill of Rights? Because King George III, abused the colonists by not allowing any of these rights. Our constitutional rights were born of our forefathers' tyranny and spilled blood. What a gift we received. May we act deserving of this gift.

Freedom once obtained, is not freedom forever secured!

If freedom is lost now to those men who would rule other men, mankind may never regain his freedom again. Why? I can answer that in one word. Technology.

Mankind has the technology that will enable one group of men to enslave the others to their end. With all the wonderful, amazing, beautiful, advancements man has made in technology, mankind has not kept up the same pace morally or ethically. All things in this universe are governed by universal principles or laws. Air flight has its principles that govern safe flight, automobiles, ships, medicine, computers, all are governed by laws, principles, and programming rules. Do we think man is no different?

The problem is we humans do not agree on the principles that govern man's behavior. Or even that there are any principles, moral or otherwise, that govern man's behavior. God placed the moral code of humanity within each of us. I do not believe in a

God who would do otherwise to us. Natural law, discoverable via human reasoning, reveals the moral code of humanity within each of us. I do not believe our existence is without any moral guideposts. That would commit us to misery without hope of escape. I believe that all humans innately know this. Most all humans have some similar and general sense of right and wrong, etc. Thomas Paine said, “As for morality the knowledge of it exists in every man’s conscience.”[31]

Thomas Paine said, “As for morality the knowledge of it exists in every man’s conscience.”

There are those that, by rejecting this notion of natural moral law, must therefore reject any universal morality of nature in order to support their arguments against absolute universal values. Perhaps they think that to do otherwise would turn them against their own argument.

Imagine denying the principles of flight in the construction of an aircraft. Are you going to get on that plane? Imagine living in an arbitrary state of subjectivism where the ruling power, ever changing, sets the rules according to whim and desire, not principle. You want to live there? Or would you rather live in the land of principle where all men are governed by their own consent and no man is the king of the other. That is the land I choose. Like my forefathers before me I find the rules that apply to man’s behavior, the natural moral law, to be self evident. I make no plans to walk down the path into the Gladys and Wonderland of subjectivism. Subjectivism and moral relativism is the land where chaos and misery reign, freedom flees, and principles are banished.

We must consider the state of man in this mix of the very wonderful and awe inspiring technology our scientists have gifted us with. We must return to the age of enlightenment, reason, saddled firmly upon high moral character. We must reaffirm, once again, the self evident principles that our forefathers so clearly recognized and used as the foundation for our country. The country that freed man on the basis of belief in self-evident God-given rights and absolute moral natural laws. If we lag behind our technology in this manner, the future of man, it seems to me, risks wielding technology that he himself created but cannot responsibly control. In a nutshell, the character of man matters and our freedom depends upon it.

The Takeaway for Freedom's Defense: The cocktail of ignorance and apathy, is freedom's enemy, the tyrants dream, and posterity's nightmare.

Chapter 5

The Hidden Branch of Government

The Assault on Freedom: Progressive regulation, transfers power and control from the citizens and the free market to the government and its bureaucrats.

Merriam-Webster defines "red tape" as "official routine or procedure marked by excessive complexity which results in delay or inaction." Others refer to red tape as regulation.

Government regulation is how you can fundamentally transform a free market capitalist customer serving system, into a socialist bureaucratic and government serving system. Regulation, beyond the very minimally necessary, shifts the power of control from the individual and his private property, the individual businesses and their respective owners, to the state and its regulating bureaucrats. Practically everything in our country is heavily regulated far beyond what is necessary. This forces business to serve the regulatory state instead of the consumer. In a free market system the customer is king and the business must cater to him or die. In a regulatory socialist state, the government is

In a free market system the customer is king and the business must cater to him or die. In a regulatory socialist state, the government is king and the business must serve this master or die.

king and the business must serve this master or die. In short, government bureaucrats and crony capitalists win, especially with large corporations that can afford to hire lobbyists to fend off (pay off), the regulators or Congressmen. The losers are individual liberty, the consumer, employees, small business, and start up or would be entrepreneurs who can't afford the price of opening a business because of regulatory restrictions.

A clear and recent example between the New York City taxi business and Uber taxi service occurred in 2015. Put another way, the free market vs. government regulation. A taxi cab in NYC must have a "medallion" or license to operate. The New York government, through the years, strictly regulated the taxi business to control the number of medallions allowed. Therefore, the cost of these medallions have sky-rocketed from a cost of hundreds of thousands of dollars to over a million dollars. The result is that a working guy cannot afford to buy a medallion and become a taxi driver. Now owning a medallion in NYC is a rich man's game and government regulation caused it. This is a direct result of government trampling the free market by regulating the number of medallions allowed. Additionally, the outrageous medallion prices translate into outrageous cab fares for the public. Enter Uber and its free market capitalist solution. All of a sudden medallion prices started dropping because customers began using Uber. Uber now has more cars in NY than traditional taxis. This is a direct and clear illustration of how free market capitalism serves us, the consumer, and how government regulation harms us and favors the bureaucrats and aids in the creation of crony capitalism. Regulation amounts to protectionism for the large corporate entities and the wealthy because they can afford teams of attorneys to jump over the regulatory hurdles. The small business guy cannot afford this option, so he is out. Regulation, as you can see from this example, is a threat to individual liberty and free market competition. Regulation aids the wealthy who can afford the million-dollar medallion price tag while it kicks the little guy out of the game entirely. Government regulation is not the friend of liberty, the American consumer or the free market. The proof? The government still attempted to strike back against the free market as NYC mayor Bill de Blasio sought to impose a moratorium (regulation) on new Uber cars for one year. Mayor de Blasio eventually backed down stating he would study the issue.[32] Chalk one up to the free market. Go Uber!

Regulation amounts to protectionism for the large corporate entities and the wealthy because they can afford teams of attorneys to jump over the regulatory hurdles.

Do not make the mistake, however, of simply concluding that regulation is not a problem because Uber and the free market prevailed in this instance. There were years where the wealthy, crony capitalists and bureaucrats dominated the taxi business in NY and the little guy and the consumer were harmed. Uber's free market victory is true, but do not forget the human tragedy left in the wake of big government regulation every day across this country. This was one victory in a war on a Red-Tape Government to free the capitalist markets once again in America.

Eventually we all become losers in the red-tape State because of the inevitable destructive regulatory bondage the bureaucrats force upon the free market. Have you seen the state of affairs in Venezuela lately, the human tragedy caused by the red-tape State of socialism? Venezuela is a current and very clear example of the human misery and suffering caused by socialism. All done, as the bureaucrat proclaims, for your good and for your safety.

Article. 1., Section. 1. of the U.S. Constitution

> "All legislative powers herein granted shall be vested in a Congress of the United States, which shall consist of a Senate and House of Representatives."

Who makes the laws according to the Constitution? Congress. Congress is called the *people's house* because it is the embodiment of the elected representatives from each of our congressional districts and respective states. For this reason, our elected officials in Congress should, it would reasonably seem, be accountable to their district's inhabitants, for the laws they pass. This, it would also seem, has the effect of keeping the representatives accountable to the people and thus, the people, in a circuitous direct way, have some say in the Federal laws that get passed.

So if the Constitution says that only the Congress can make laws, what about the regulations? Who is making all the hundreds of thousands of regulations and are regulations the same as laws? Moreover, if they are the same as laws why isn't the Congress the one making the regulations? All good questions and I will do my best to answer each of them. The following is a word from John Locke in 1689 on this very issue.

> The Legislative cannot transfer the Power of Making Laws to any other hands. For it being but a delegated Power from the People, they, who have it, cannot pass it over to others. . . And when the people have said, "We will submit to rules, and be governed by Laws made by such Men, and in such Forms, no Body else can say other Men shall make Laws for them; nor can the people be bound by any Laws but such as are Enacted by those, whom they have Chosen, and Authorized to make Laws for them. The power of the Legislative being derived from the People by a positive voluntary Grant and Institution, can be no other, than what the positive Grant conveyed, which being only to make Laws, and not to make Legislators, the Legislative can have no power to transfer their Authority of making laws, and place it in other hands.
>
> John Locke, *Two Treatises of Government*, Chapter XI, Section 141

But this is exactly what Congress has done. It passes off the authority to regulate us, to the many regulatory agencies. Nameless un-elected, un-accountable, often lifetime, bureaucrats. A question; if your job is to create regulations for the shoe industry what will happen if you can't think of any more regulations to write? You can either stop regulating and lose your job, or think of something about the shoe business to continually regulate. Only a person of high moral integrity will choose the former. The former being the choice of liberty for all, rather than job for self, and regulatory bondage for all. It's called loving your neighbor as you love yourself. The irony? Loving your neighbor as yourself also serves your best interest. Ponder that. It is crucial to our liberty. In a country where there is liberty only for some, there is actually liberty for none. Government never puts itself out of business so it will continue to regulate way beyond the minimally necessary. Government regulations are the product of bureaucrats just as inventions and consumer goods are the product of the free market. Which one do you think is trying to provide for your needs and desires, the capitalist or the bureaucrat? We are a country in regulatory crisis due to unelected bureaucrats passing by fiat tens of thousands of rules that we and industry must comply with. Moreover, our congressmen and women get to pretend innocent because they didn't actually write all the regulations, the bureaucrat regulators did. We are a country being run and overrun by Federal Regulations. An expansive Federal Government means a less free people. We are living in a veritable world of red tape.

Government regulations are the product of bureaucrats just as inventions and consumer goods are the product of the free market.

The Pew Research Center, in an article about Congressional productivity, cites the 113th Congress as having passed 165 laws in 2013-2014; the 112th Congress as having passed 174 laws in 2011-2012; and the 111th Congress as having passed 237 laws in 2009-2010.[33]

Next comes the "regulatory phase" of lawmaking. This is the creation of tens of thousands of rules by bureaucrats, not Congress, to enforce the laws Congress passed. Lawyers will argue the difference between laws and rules or regulations, but for you and me there is essentially no difference. All must be complied with according to the Federal Government. Therefore, rules, regulations, mandates, can all be seen as laws we must obey. There is distinction in name only, the import is the same. This is done by federal regulatory agencies like the FDA (Food and Drug Administration, SEC (Securities and Exchange Commission), FCC (Federal Communications Commission), BLM (Bureau of Land Management), EPA Environmental Protection Agency, and on and on and on. Some regulatory agency exists to regulate just about everything in our lives. To this end the Competitive Enterprise Institute, a Washington Watchdog organization, reports that in 2011 there were 81,247 pages of regulations or rules added to the Federal Register. In 2012 there were 78,961 more federal regulation pages added, and in 2013 there were yet another 79,311 pages of Red Tape added. In the decade of 2,000's there were 730,176 pages of federal regulations or rules directed at Americans and businesses of all types, etc.[34] In the past 20 years there have been about 1.5 million pages of regulations added to the Federal Register. Who could even know how to obey all these rules? These are only the federal regulations. There are also all the state and local regulations and regulators.

The government does not make your clothes, cars, smart phones, books, etc. the free market does. The capitalist is trying to supply your needs and product desires while the government is busy regulating him.

This goes on year after year after year. Keep in mind that the expansive federal bureaucracy has been growing rapidly since the Progressive Era began in about 1913. That is over one hundred years of heavy regulation of our lives and our economy. You will hear big government statists, and progressives attempt to blame capitalism for the problems that plague our economy at this time. This is not true and the facts bear that out.

Moral capitalism built America and the bureaucrats are putting it into the bondage of regulation which favors the government control of our lives, the wealthy, and large corporations. Regulation hurts the small guy and limits competition which hurts the consumer. This shifts the power of self-determination from the individual and the free market to the government. The government does not make your clothes, cars, smart phones, books, etc. the free market does. The capitalist is trying to supply your needs and product desires while the government is busy regulating him. We are experiencing the fallout of progressive government overregulation in our economy right now. Heavy regulation burdens an economy, slows it down and increases product cost. It will eventually all but kill an economy if it is not pushed back.

Look at Cuba, Venezuela, N. Korea, Greece, and the European Union (EU), etc. It is a vicious cycle because the bureaucrats use the slowdowns as reason to offer more "government help" to get out of the slowdown. This cycle repeats over and over and over. Ask yourself a simple question. In America's heydays of growth and expansion and during the industrial revolution, was she heavily regulated or free to conduct free-enterprise? Was liberty king or the red-tape government? The unfettered human spirit coupled with the entrepreneurial spirit of enterprising Americans provides the goods and services that we desire for the lifestyle that we enjoy, not the government. American capitalism is still providing these things for us in spite of the state of red-tape bureaucracy, albeit at higher prices because of the regulation. But it cannot do this forever. And it is costlier and more difficult than ever, especially for low-budgeted startups. In other words, the average guy. The invisible hand of regulation has been taking its toll far too long now and our economy is injured as a result. Most of us are aware of the poor state of our economy in the recent decade. Moreover, the regulation hurts the little guy the most. How? By creating expensive regulatory hurdles that the typical start-up business or individual entrepreneurs can't afford. Result, the little guy is out of business before he even gets started. And, competition is limited thus hurting the consumer. Why? Because when you limit competition prices rise and quality is decreased. Competition drives the market toward better products and lower prices. Just keep reading and I think you will agree

Government, by contrast, provides nothing for the American consumer. It's not its job to do so, but neither is its job to obstruct, via regulation, the efforts of the free market, and that is exactly what I think it is doing by all the hyper-regulating of our lives. The Uber example shows this is happening. The government is a net taker of the fruits of our labor. It kicks nothing into the economic pot. It takes from the economic pot. The cost of regulation to American businesses and individuals is approximately two trillion dollars per year just to obey the regulations imposed by the government. The government, (state, local, and federal), then takes approximately six trillion dollars in taxes and fees from the American people and business.[35] That is a total of EIGHT TRILLION DOLLARS. Imagine if half or more of that eight trillion dollars was given back each year? What would that do for you and our economy? We are talking about 80 + trillion dollars in the cost of government for every 10 years of our lives at current rates of taxation and compliance cost. Is it any

Competition drives the market toward better products and lower prices.

wonder that we have economic problems? The government is our economic problem! For additional perspective consider that in fiscal 2016 Wal-Mart had a revenue of only 482+ billion; State Grid 329 + billion; Royal Dutch Shell brought in 272+ billion. No corporation takes in *trillions* of dollars like the U.S. Government does. It is not even close. Keep in mind that the above cited companies produced and sold their products to the consumer for their profits. The consumer got something and the corporation got something. The U.S. government, by contrast, took by taxation trillions of dollars from the hard working American citizens and it produces nothing more than more government bureaucrats and regulation. Not to be misunderstood, the government certainly has a constitutional role and it needs money to do that, but it has clearly usurped that role and it is operating far beyond its enumerated constitutional role. The government's constitutional role in brief, is to secure our individual liberty and freedom. Its role is not to hinder and limit our freedom by enacting massive piles and pages of regulations for us to live by. Regulation, at some point, breaches the very limits of its defined role and then government becomes a threat to the very

> *Regulation, at some point, breaches the very limits of its defined role and then government becomes a threat to the very liberty it is supposed to be protecting.*

liberty it is supposed to be protecting. This constitutional breach of government has long been passed.

Here is a small sample of what we are getting for all this regulation and oversight. Remember, as you read, all regulation is said to be for our safety, health, and security. So here we go, from the CDC.gov website itself. The FDA is heavily regulating the food and pharmaceutical industries for our safety yet hospitalizations and deaths 2000-2008 are; by bacteria Campylobacter spp. 850,000 hospitalizations and 76 deaths each year; Salmonella spp. 1,000,000 hospitalizations and 380 deaths per year; Parasite Toxoplasma gondii 87,000 hospitalizations and 330 deaths per year; Virus, Norovirus 5,500,000 hospitalizations and 150 deaths per year.[36]

On the FDA.gov website under FAERS (Federal Adverse Event Reporting System) the following was found regarding adverse drug events, therapeutic biologic products, and medication error reports. The deaths or other serious outcomes by year are as follows:

- 2010 - 82,704 deaths and serious outcomes
- 2011 - 98,469 deaths and serious outcomes
- 2012 - 117,202 deaths and serious outcomes
- 2013 - 116,330 deaths and serious outcomes
- 2014 - 123,927 deaths and serious outcomes[37]

Notice the annual increase in the number of deaths and serious events. The medical industry is certainly one of the most heavily regulated but the apparent benefit of regulation to the public does not bode well. America has some of the best doctors and medical care in the world and this is not to be critical of our doctors or the medical industry. The only point here is that we cannot regulate utopian outcomes. Whether it is crime, product quality, health and security, etc.

Just two more areas of regulation to discuss and we will move past numbers and annual stats. I wanted to avoid two forms of writing in this project but I have found it impossible to do so. The two areas I wanted to avoid were statistics and sports analogies so please bear with me we are almost done.

Chicago has gun regulations and laws that are among the strictest in the country. Yet the New York online magazine reports, in a March 29, 2016, article, "the murder rate in Chicago is up 84 percent this year."[38] Chicagotribune.com reports 490 murders in 2015 in Chicago, and 2016 ended with 762 murders also in Chicago.[39] A good case could be made that gun regulations in Chicago have signaled to the criminally minded that the law abiding innocent public is unarmed—making Chicago a free crime zone! Regulation can't stop murder. That is the job of the human heart. Morality trumps regulation.

Have you ever heard of Abigail Krustinger? A few years back Forbes.com had an article about this four-year-old child and her "lemonade stand." In Coralville, Iowa, police shut down her lemonade stand. Her father said she didn't make more than five dollars. She was trying to raise money for a bicycle race across Iowa.[40] Another nearby stand was also closed and the police informed the parent that the appropriate permit would cost $400.00. A $400.00 permit cost effectively shuts down the lemonade stand business of the entrepreneurial child. Does this sound like a government in favor of capitalism? Is this what a capitalist bureaucrat lawmaker would spend his day doing? Does shutting down a child's lemonade stand protect your liberty and make you or your child safe? I offer the same question in the matter of Uber?

In Georgia, the police shut down a lemonade stand that three girls were running in order to save money to get into the local water park. The police also said the girls need a business license, food permit, and a peddler's permit to operate. The same Forbes.com article goes on to say that "food trucks are also under the gun of regulators and city governments across the country." The Forbes.com article also says the list goes on and on and even cited the problem "government officials calling cops on kids for selling cupcakes."

These child capitalist entrepreneurs have every right to do what they were doing. I had a lemonade stand when I was a kid as did thousands of other kids in the 1960s. The government wouldn't dare try this stunt back then. Americans would have never stood for it. Lemonade stands are a good way for children to begin to learn free market capitalism, the value of working, the cost to make an item, and what it takes to sell at a profit, pleasing your customers, etc. Much good has been done through the past years with American kids running lemonade stands and much harm is being done presently by these over regulating bureaucrats. Is this the country you want? I don't.

Alexis de Tocqueville stated the following in his book *Democracy in America* in 1835.

> Above this race of men (We the people) stands an immense and tutelary power (self appointed rulers)... it seeks on the contrary to keep them in perpetual childhood... the only arbiter of that happiness: it provides for their security, foresees and supplies their necessities, facilitates their pleasures, manages their principal concerns, directs their industry, regulates the descent of property, and subdivides their inheritances-what remains, but to spare them all the care of thinking and all the trouble of living?...The principle of equality has prepared men for these things: ... It covers the surface of society with a network of small complicated rules, minute and uniform, through which the most original minds and the most energetic characters cannot penetrate, to rise above the crowd... till each nation is reduced to be nothing better than a flock of timid and industrial animals, of which the government is the shepherd.[41]

Tocqueville goes on, speaking of government regulation, to call it servitude. I hope you are beginning to see the point here, government cannot regulate or legislate our safety, our health, and prosperity, no matter how valiant the effort may seem. What the misguided regulatory effort to control human behavior ends up accomplishing is, placing each of us, free market capitalism, and our country in red-tape bondage, economic duress, and beholden to the government. This is the eventual doom of socialistic systems and history is replete with many tragic examples as is the present, i.e. Venezuela, for example again.

Europe is part of America's past because America held high the banner of individual freedom and individual rights, not Europe. We left the old world and created a new and free world. But there are those who desire to compare the two and declare we should be more like Europe. Therefore, I thought I would include a few examples of regulatory brilliance from the EU (European Union). Keep in mind as you read that regulations come from some bureaucrat sitting in an office pondering ways to protect our security and safety. From the movie, *Brexit*, Enjoy!

- Some bureaucrat came up with 454 regulations about *towels*.
- Another bureaucrat came up with 1,246 regulations about *bread*.
- In an adjacent bureaucrat's office another 172 regulations were thought of for *mirrors*.
- Yet another hard working bureaucrat came up with 118 ways to regulate *shampoo*.
- *Coffee*, a particular favorite of the red-tapers, gets 625 regulations.
- Everybody loves *dogs* so they get 556 regulations to better their lives.
- Can't have *soup* without a regulated *spoon* so its gets 210 rules.

- Did you brush your teeth today? Good because your *toothbrush* got 47 regulations.
- *Got Milk?* It should be good and half or less its current cost because it is the all time winner of our list with 12,653 regulations to make it better, safer, and guaranteed more expensive because of the regulatory process the producers and retailers must deal with before it ever gets to your refrigerator.

I'm sure there is a part of you that, like me, wants to chuckle at this stuff. But it is no laughing matter. It costs businesses millions of dollars just to "obey" the regulators. Then you, the consumer, pay the tab at the retail counter. Not to mention the loss of jobs due to money spent on regulation compliance instead of hiring new employees. Bureaucratic statists will never stop the regulation process. This regulatory process has the effect of removing, almost without notice, the power and freedom of the individual over his own life and property, and transferring it to the power of the state. The state then begins to determine what that individual can and cannot do. Just like Tocqueville said back in 1835. Did you know that the agreement document Great Britain signed in order to get into the EU took two grown men to carry into the room for the signing ceremony. This large stack of paper appears to be almost three feet high as well. God gives us 10 simple commandments, and man gives us countless thousands of regulations.

Life is an adventure full of risk. Neither you nor the red-tape man in Washington can do a thing about it. Can you guarantee you own absolute safety? Safety from accident, injury, bankruptcy, death, etc. No you cannot. Man does not have absolute control over these matters. Man lives at risk. It's called life. So, why would you think that a regulation on a piece of paper can have some miraculous positive contribution to your life? If you can't have full authority over your own safety and welfare, what makes you think a bureaucrat can?

Who has the greatest interest in your health, safety, and happiness? You, your neighbor, or the bureaucrat who does not even know your name or that you exist? Let's say you are a restaurant owner. Who do you think has the greater interest in the cleanliness of your operation and the satisfaction of your customers? Who do you think will be impacted most severely by a Salmonella outbreak? You or the bureaucrat? So do you keep your restaurant clean and your employees aware of that need because you are afraid of a fine from the bureaucrat or because a Salmonella outbreak could cause harm to your customers and financial devastation for you and your family.

Can you see, by way of this example, the Uber example, and the lemonade stand, that the free market does not need the bureaucrat. The bureaucrat is more of a burden to society than a help. If you don't keep a good, safe, and clean restaurant the free market will regulate you right out of business. This is true of all areas of business. Capitalism has contained within its natural structure the best and most efficient system of regulation. It is the consumer, you and me. If a product is of poor quality, you won't buy it and the businessman is out. If it is unsafe or too expensive, the market will not buy it either. If a product injures you, you then have recourse through the tort (legal) system. You can sue for damages. The free market must have the consumer to survive, therefore it always strives to offer the best product quality and cost value to its customers. It must serve you or die. Make sense? A business will live or die by the free market according to the way it treats its customers.

One more idea to ponder. Let's say you love your healthy and able parents and your healthy children more than anything in the world and I hope you do. Because of your love and concern for their safety and happiness, however, you present each of them with a list of rules that they must live by for their own good. You do this with well-meaning intentions. Not things like be honest, be helpful, respectful of others, in other words not a list of moral virtues. Rather, you give them a specific list of rules and mandates and insist on full compliance. Rules like how to get out of bed without injury, rules on where rugs are to be safely place in the home, rules on how to shower safely, rules on how much water they are to consume each day, rules for the 18 inches minimal distance between furniture items in the home (it's true, watch *Brexit*, the movie), regulations for exact portions of food for meals, etc. While you are declaring your love and concern for their safely and happiness I think they would look at you like you are crazy. Furthermore, they would not see your act as love at all but rather restrictive and a denial of their freedom and their own sense of responsibility. They would probably also be insulted at the apparent arrogance you portend for even imagining having such authority and nonsense. Lastly, I think you would be laughed out of the room. Risk cannot be regulated out of life, but freedom can.

Risk cannot be regulated out of life, but freedom can.

I can't avoid a baseball analogy because it makes clear point of the matter. The following are the four ways to play the game of baseball. Of the four, I ask you to choose which is best for the game, the players, owners, referees, and the fans.

1. THE NO RULES version of baseball. In this version of the game there are simply "no rules." Now ask yourself what level of competition would this result in? What level of enjoyment for the fans, players, owners, even the refs would there be? Would the fans stay and watch such a game? No, not likely. The game would have no real appeal and thus the game would not be able to stay in business.
2. THE RIGHT BALANCE OF MINIMAL RULES AND MORAL version of baseball. In this version, the game has maximum excitement because the players have only a

minimum of rules to play by. Therefore, they are free to play the game to their peak ability. This environment also cultivates maximum competition between the players and the teams. The stadium is full every game because of its fun and exciting competition. The fans, players, referees, and owners alike all enjoy the game of baseball. The game has a nice, exciting pace to it, and everyone respects the rules of play. Everyone wins in this version of baseball. The stadium is full and so are the bank accounts. All are happy.

3. THE TOO MANY RULES version of baseball. Now imagine so many rules and regulations that players are hardly able to play the game. The referees even argue about the complexity and endless rules. Practically all competition is gone from the game because there are so many rules the players can hardly move without some violation of compliance. The fans begin to boo and leave the stadium. Play is slowed to a crawl and has become extremely boring. It seems as though the competition is more between the referees arguing about which rule to apply than between the players who are actually playing the game. The truth is that there isn't much play going on at all. The game begins to die, owners and players lose money as fans lose interest and leave the stadium. The game has been regulated almost to death and will soon die if this does not change.

4. THE RIGHT BALANCE OF RULES BUT IMMORAL version of baseball. In version 2 above, the unstated but implied or assumed presence of the natural moral law was doing its job. All played by and respected the rules. Now imagine that the field is full of players and referees all having the tendency to cheat when they can. The game becomes chaotic once again. There is more arguing than playing of the game. Competition takes a serious downturn. Interest in the game is lost. And the bank accounts of all involved go into serious decline as the fans leave the stadium once again. You see, the right balance of rules is only one of two critical components that is needed. You also have to have morality and integrity of character within the players, referees, and the owners. This is critical for peak performance, healthy competition, and the overall excitement and integrity and sustainability of the game.

It should be clear that Version No. 2 above is the best scenario for the game. Now instead of baseball, think of capitalism with the same four versions. Version 2 is the best for baseball and capitalism. The progressive statist would have you and the public believe that the capitalist and capitalism seeks the no rules version 1 above. They want you to believe that a chaotic greedy free for all is what capitalism is all about, therefore, it must be highly regulated to avoid this outcome. This is absolutely false and the very history of America is a testament to this being a false claim.

This false claim, however, is the basis upon the socialist bureaucrats attempt to build consensus for his desire to regulate, which is his true aim. Regulation is the progressive's tool to fundamentally transform a capitalist system into a socialist system. Therefore, the degree of regulation is critical to monitor in order to maintain a capitalistic system. We do not have a capitalistic system today. We have been regulated into a government run system rather than a free market run system. Do you remember the lemonade stand? Overregulation of our lives and businesses is destroying our economy, country, and the American Dream. We Americans have, in many ways, replaced morality with government regulation. Or put another way America has shifted, in large measure, from belief in God, morality, and individual liberty as the solution to our lives and problems, to government and regulation as being our savior. Add to this, the systemic moral corruption and you have a once great nation well into decline. Freedom, decent moral values, and the unfettered human spirit built America. Progressive socialist red-tape bureaucracy and immorality is destroying her.

Regulation is the progressive's tool to fundamentally transform a capitalist system into a socialist system.

When America's government is down to regulating lemonade stands against the interests of its children, America cannot be said to be a free country where the people are free to pursue their happiness. Do you think an American capitalist-leaning bureaucrat thought of all those regulations for the lemonade stands? Or do you think a socialist-leaning bureaucrat thought of and enforced those regulations for the lemonade stands. What would happen if a homeless person decided to open a small lemonade stand and sell a cool drink of lemonade to passersby rather than simply begging. The government would shut him down for not having the regulated permit. That is what would happen. The homeless person cannot afford the permits so he cannot go into business. Government regulations have him blocked out of the system. To a homeless person who wants to participate in America and at least try to provide a service and earn enough to buy his daily food, this would be a huge benefit. And how many Americans would buy a cup just to support his effort—a lot of Americans would. If the socialist bureaucrat has the time to regulate lemonade stands, what do you think it has been doing to all the small businesses across this great land? Again, we are more socialist than capitalist. I hope you can see by these few examples what socialist regulation does to an economy and people. It places them in red-tape bondage, thwarts the pursuit of happiness and harms our economy. The individual eventually loses the autonomy to pursue his own happiness.

America, we need to wake up. The progressive-statist would have you not know or think about this so he can keep blaming the country's economic woes on capitalism. But we are no longer a free market capitalist nation.

Socialism is regulation that never stops until it destroys its hosts—free market capitalism and individual freedom.

Here is the big secret. Our economic woes are due to the forced socialist regulations that have been oozing through and permeating American business for more than a hundred years now. Not to mention the national debt incurred to pay for progressive government social programs and the confiscatory tax rates. Ever since the progressive big government era began around 1913. Our economy and people are experiencing the economic fallout of a government controlled red-tape socialist state. The difference between socialism and capitalism is nothing more than the degree of government regulation. With a few minimal rules, free honest people and markets, you have capitalism. Way too many rules create government controlled socialism. This does not mean that the red-tape bureaucrats will taper or stop their regulating. Once these bureaucrats have control the socialist regulating never stops. It will continue and things will get worse and that is not the fault of capitalism. Socialism is regulation that never stops until it destroys its hosts—free market capitalism and individual freedom.

The Takeaway for Freedom's Defense: The power to regulate is the power to destroy.

Chapter 6

Money

The Assault on Freedom: Progressives gutted our money by removing its store of value - gold. In exchange we were given fiat currency which they endlessly print, causing it to lose value. This is why many of us never seem to get ahead.

> "Paper is poverty. It is only the ghost of money and not money itself."
>
> Thomas Jefferson in a letter to Edward Carrington, 1788

What is money? Suppose I said to you that the fancy paper with numbers on it that the government prints and the metal coins in your pocket are not money. Moreover, both the metal coins and the printed paper used to be money but now they are not. By now you are probably wondering, ok what's the catch? Next I tell you that the U. S. government removed America's money from its citizens, yes, you too, with hardly a whimper from the unsuspecting public. It occurred with little more than a nominal blip on a fiscal radar screen.

Hold on because it gets worse. Americans were told for decades to open a savings account to save those fancy printed pieces of paper and metal coins. They were told to save for the future. It sounded reasonable, if not darn good advice, so no one really questioned it. Well, most of the general public didn't question it.

While trusting Americans were busy working hard and saving for their futures, the U.S. government began in earnest to decouple America's money supply from the gold standard. This process began in earnest back in 1913 under the Woodrow Wilson Administration. Essentially, it all started with President Woodrow Wilson's creation of the Federal Reserve central banking system, the ratification of the Sixteenth Amendment to the Constitution in order to tax your income (which is a labor tax and therefore a tax on your time), and the Internal Revenue Service (established to impose and enforce a capitation or direct taxation on U.S Citizens). In other words, a tax on you. This was the beginning of the statist-progressive era of big government in America. This was also the beginning of the loss of real money in America. One should keep in mind the American job was the entryway to wealth building for the typical American. A job was the golden ticket to the gateway of the American dream. This is a major part of what fueled the American industrial revolution of the nineteenth century. America, the place where a man could truly keep the fruits of his labor, and therefore a real chance to improve

A job was the golden ticket to the gateway of the American dream.

life for his family as well as himself. Moreover, the possibility of saving seed money for that dream business or to fund a new invention idea became a reality for the average person. Word of this great news swept the globe. The American dream became a reality and America became the beacon of hope throughout the world. America offered speech freedom, religious freedom, and the freedom to pursue happiness (dreams) because it offered economic freedom. People the world over clamored to find their way through Ellis Island.

To tax a man's labor by taking part of the money he works for is bondage because time is required to make the money. Another way to think of the income tax is a time tax, because you are being taxed on the time you spend in life working. Also, there was no income tax from the founding of America in 1791 (the year the Constitution was ratified), until President Woodrow Wilson in 1913. Why? Because the founders were against any income tax, direct tax, or capitation. Capitation or direct taxation is a tax on the person and his or her time. The founders were adamantly against this and therefore, they instituted no income tax. Did you know that? The founders as well as the colonists dealt with tax tyranny from the King of England, King George III. The American Revolution was fought largely over this issue and general governmental tyranny. Therefore, the last thing the founders would consider doing would be to impose the same or similar tax tyranny upon the American people. They had just victoriously rebelled against this. Imagine that there was no income tax today and you received your full pay on payday. That's how it was for Americans until the progressives started their progressive income tax in 1913.

> "A wise and frugal government, which shall restrain men from injuring one another, shall leave them otherwise free to regulate their own pursuits of industry and improvement, and *shall not take from the mouth of labor the bread it has earned.*" (Italics added)
>
> Thomas Jefferson, First Inaugural March 4, 1801 [42]

In *The Spirit of Laws* written in 1748, Montesquieu says, "A capitation (tax) is more natural to slavery; a duty (tax) on merchandise is more natural to liberty, by reason it has not so direct a relation to the person."[43]

Thomas Jefferson copied this into his Commonplace Book "no capitation, or other direct, tax shall be laid..." Article I Section 9 United States Constitution.

While the process of devaluing America's money began with the massive growth of government by the Wilson administration, this was only the beginning. The complete process took place over many years and wasn't final until the fateful day of Sunday, August 15, 1971. That was the day the Nixon administration kicked the last leg from under the table of the American gold standard. This was the day money died in America and currency, the ghost of money, appeared. We will discuss this later in this chapter, but for now I want to return to the original question of, what is money?

MONEY IS:

- A medium of exchange
- A unit of account
- divisible
- portable
- durable
- fungible
- MONEY IS A STORE OF VALUE

CURRENCY IS:

- All of the above
- EXCEPT A STORE OF VALUE

What is in your pocket is not money because the store of value has been removed. What you have is called fiat currency. Paper dollars with *no* store of value. Fiat means: *An arbitrary decree.* So, the government simply decreeing that a piece of paper with numbers on it makes it money. No, it does not. The magic wand of government waved over a piece of fancy paper does nothing. If this were true, I have one question to ask. Why then were we ever on the gold standard in the first place? Because paper is paper and gold is money. Gold and silver have been used for money for over 5,000 years of human history.

> "The modern banking system manufactures money (fiat currency) out of nothing, the process is perhaps the most astounding piece of sleight of hand that was ever invented."
>
> Sir Josiah Charles Stamp, Director of the Bank of England, 1920s [44]

Let's now define the terms that make up money.

- A medium of exchange means your money will be accepted for an item that you want to purchase.
- A unit of account means the money can be counted and so it has a numerical value on each piece.
- Divisible simply means it can be divided.
- Portable means it can be carried from place to place.
- Durable means that it lasts a reasonably long time.
- Fungible means the dollar in your hand is the same as the dollar in mine.
- Most importantly money is a store of value. This is why the founders established the gold standard for America's money supply.

Now let's see what the Constitution has to say about money. In Article I Section 10 it says, "No State shall... emit Bills of Credit; make anything but gold and silver coin as tender in payment of debts."

> "History records that the money changers have used every form of abuse, intrigue, deceit, and violent means possible to maintain their control over governments by controlling money and its issuance."
>
> James Madison[45]

Now that you have learned what money is and what it is not and that America used to have money but now it does not, you should be asking why? First, it is important to understand what the purpose of the gold standard was to begin with. The gold standard was put in place to protect the "store of value" of the citizens and therefore the country's printed paper dollars. Also, the gold standard prevented the government from simply printing play money or un-backed fiat paper dollars for things it wanted to spend it on. This kept politicians from promising a new this or that government program because they were not allowed to simply print money to fund the programs. The money supply (amount of paper currency in existence) was intentionally and constitutionally limited because the U.S. gold supply was limited, and the dollar was purposefully tied to gold as the constitution requires. In other words, this gold connection protected the dollar's store of value which in turn protected the citizen's ability to maintain and increase his or her personal wealth. Each dollar stood for a certain amount of gold that the government actually had in its vaults. A 20 dollar bill was at one time called a 20 dollar Gold Certificate and could be exchanged at the bank for a 1 oz. (.9765) $20 dollar gold coin, a St. Gaudins. There were Silver Certificates also and these could be traded in at the bank for the equivalent amount of silver in coins. A one-dollar paper silver certificate could be exchanged for a one-dollar silver coin. It was called a silver dollar, I had them when I was a child. Can you imagine walking in to your local bank and doing that today?

Why did the American government do this? You see, the gold standard placed fiscal restraint (financial responsibility) upon the federal government. It could not grow and expand because it could not print more money than the country had in the gold supply. If the government wanted a greater money supply it had to then obtain more gold. This gold standard was a constitutional restraint upon the government from growing beyond its means and putting the public in debt. So what did the government do to get around this? It got rid of the gold standard. In my view, this act was the true beginning of the end of "Government for the people, by the people" in America. With the creation of the Federal Reserve (a private central bank) the government began to print more currency than it had in gold. It simply started printing currency in order to pay for and create social programs that helped statist-progressive politicians get and remain elected. It did this to fund war as well. It is crucial to note that when government prints money it is thereby creating debt that the citizens must pay back via taxation. We have squandered our gold standard for a nation in debt.

Thomas Jefferson said, "I believe that banking institutions are more dangerous to our liberties than standing armies."[46]

Before long the government had printed more dollars than the corresponding gold it had in the vault. Thus, the progressives forced the hand, so to speak, of the country to get off the gold standard. By printing excessive numbers of dollars far beyond the available gold supply in the vaults it created a crisis of sorts. Now, if too many people wanted to trade their dollars for gold the government didn't have enough gold to meet their promise. Solution, get rid of the standard. And, this my fellow Americans, is why you used to have money, but now you do not.

The gold standard melded or joined gold to the paper. This protected your dollar from being eaten alive by inflation due to the excessive and unconstitutional printing of fiat currency. Fiat currency places the public on a monetary treadmill, so to speak.

You run and run but you are never allowed to catch the carrot. The consequences to the U.S. citizens and to the country itself are truly tragic. The U.S. dollar has lost more than 97% of its value since President Woodrow Wilson, in 1913, created the Federal Reserve.

> Since the creation of the Federal Reserve in 1913, the dollar has lost over 97 percent of its purchasing power, the US economy has been subjected to a series of painful Federal Reserve created recessions and depressions, and government has grown to dangerous levels thanks to the Fed's policy of monetizing the debt (printing money to pay the debt). Yet the Federal Reserve still operates under a congressionally created shroud of secrecy.
>
> Ron Paul, Institute for Peace and Prosperity

The subsequent removal of the dollar from the gold standard occurred when Franklin D. Roosevelt, in 1933 on April 5, signed executive order #6102 which criminalized the possession of gold.

> By virtue of the authority vested in me by Section 5(b) of the Act of October 6, 1917, as amended by Section 2 of the Act of March 9, 1933, entitled "An act to provide relief in the existing national emergency in banking, and for other purposes, "in which amendatory Act Congress declared that a serious emergency exists, I, Franklin D. Roosevelt, President of the United States of America, do declare that said national emergency still continues to exist and pursuant to said section do hereby prohibit the hoarding of gold coin, gold bullion, and gold certificates within the continental United States by individuals, partnerships, associations and corporations...
>
> Franklin D. Roosevelt

President Roosevelt did this even though the Constitution of the United States, Article I sec. 10 clearly states: "No state shall...

make anything but gold and silver coin a tender in payment of debts...

You should know this only removed the gold standard from the dollar for the U.S. citizens in the continental U.S. America remained on the international gold standard for a while longer. But the fix was in and assured by the progressive politician because the same game of print more dollars than we have in gold was in play. The outcome was certain; it was only a matter of time.

Nevertheless, in 1944, America's dollar became the world's reserve currency at the Bretton Woods conference in New Hampshire. By 1965 the silver certificates were gone and so was silver coinage. The dollar became simple paper, and the coins became base metal.

Later in 1965, French President Charles de Gaulle warns the world that the U.S. is printing too many dollars. He was right. He further warns of an impending monetary crisis. Finally, on August 15, 1971, President Nixon removes America from the international gold standard. This was the death of paper money in America. The world is now entirely running on purely fiat currencies. This is how we got all of our socialist social programs and our current $20 plus trillion-dollar debt. We must demand a return to fiscal principle and sanity. A monetary crisis of epic proportion is coming due to the malfeasance and irresponsible fiscal actions by our government. This crisis will be an opportunity, as practically all problems are, to demand a return to the gold standard and sound

George Washington said "No generation has a right to contract debts greater than can be paid off during the course of its own existence."

money. It will also be an opportunity, as practically all problems are, for the charlatans and statists to try and convince you that more government is needed to solve the problem. It should be clear, however, that government created this problem in the first place. We will choose the path that reflects our inner selves and our knowledge of the matter. The path we choose will be the path our children walk.

George Washington said "No generation has a right to contract debts greater than can be paid off during the course of its own existence."[47]

As you read the following as well as consider the import of this chapter, a healthy appreciation of the wisdom of our Founders for establishing the gold standard in the first place should not be underestimated. Beginning in 1913 America began down a progressive or socialist path of big government spending, regulation, and tax on income. The progressive income tax. We are living the result of those big government decisions today. The departure of the gold standard in order to endlessly print debt for socialist government programs and war, has severely indebted and crippled our nation. As was stated earlier the U.S. dollar has lost over 97% of its value since 1913. Think of it this way. If a person worked for a dollar per hour for 100 hours he would have 100 dollars, right? He wants to buy a radio that cost 100 dollars but he delays his purchase for a while. The radio now cost 125 dollars so he can't buy it. He just lost 25 hours of his labor at the increased price because he must now work an additional 25 hours to make up the difference in price. The gold standard is designed to prevent us from losing the stored value that is supposed to be in our claim check on our labor (paper currency) due to inflation. The 100 dollars in paper currency in this example is like a claim check for your labor that you did to earn it. Now your claim check will not buy the radio because your claim check went down in value. When the radio went up in cost your claim check (100 dollar bill) went down. You just lost a part of your labor. Another way of understanding this is that if your grandparents kept $100,000 dollars under the mattress in 1913 and you discovered it today, and America had remained on the gold standard, the buying power of that $100,000 dollars today, given the current price of gold, would be equivalent to $6,375,000. Instead, it is now only worth about $3,000 fiat dollars in today's value. Another way to view this is: if your grandparents had hidden away $5,000 1+-oz. gold coins in 1913 ($20 each X 5,000 gold coins = $100,000) instead of paper dollars under the mattress and you discovered it today you would have approximately $6,375,000. (5,000 gold 1+-oz. coins X $1,275 price per oz.) Yes, it's correct. MILLION, over 6 of them.

The removal of the U.S. dollar gold standard was the greatest bank robbery in the history of America—but the ironic twist of the story is—the United States Government and Federal Reserve Bank robbed YOU!

> "If the American people understood the banking system they would revolt."
>
> Henry Ford[48]

We must return to a constitutional monetary system backed by a store of value such as gold and silver as instituted by our founders. The founders did this for the protection of the citizens of the United States against the self-serving politician, powerful bankers, and financiers. Their wisdom stands in stark contrast to what we have allowed to become of our countries monetary system.

"But if you want to continue as the slaves of bankers and pay the cost of your own slavery, let them continue to create money and control credit."[49] Sir Josiah Stamp, Director Bank of England

The Takeaway for Freedom's Defense: Money maintains its value against rising prices while fiat currency loses value against rising prices—by design!

Chapter 7

Socialism, Capitalism, and Thanksgiving

The Assault on Freedom: Capitalism is accused of being a greed-based economic system favoring the wealthy few, while socialism is said to be a benevolent system of wealth sharing for all.

What is capitalism? Statists, progressives, socialists, Marxists, and communists often say capitalism is a greed-based economic system that only serves the interest of the corporation and the individually wealthy. A coldhearted dollar-driven system of profit and greed. A system that creates the *haves* and *have-nots*. A system that exploits the workers and rewards the greedy corporations and wealthy individual capitalists. This is what Karl Marx thought about capitalism. Greed, moreover, is said of some notable capitalists and capitalist-supporting economists to be a good thing. Is it? Is greed a good thing? And is capitalism based upon greed? If capitalism is a good economic system, then how can it be truly based upon a vice such as greed? Can a vice, then, be also a virtue? Let's explore these notions. It is necessary to turn back to the pages of history to America's Pilgrims and the Colonial era. We will begin with a short synopsis the true story of the Pilgrims. The true version that you may have never been taught.

In the year 1620 the Pilgrims, or planters as they were called by their financial backers, having limited financial resources, entered into a contract with several merchant adventurers in London, England. The Pilgrims, had little choice but to secure the financial aid of several merchant adventurers to fund their flight from tyranny to freedom in America. Per contract the Pilgrims were to work the land in America in common with one another. All of the land and the fruits of their labor were to be held in common with no individual ownership. As payment for their transport to the new world, and for their basic life necessities, any profit would go to the merchant adventurers but none to the planters. The merchant adventurers were essentially investors seeking to profit off of the labor of the Pilgrims and would become the owners of the fruits of the labor of the Pilgrims. The merchant adventurers contractually imposed this type of economic model upon Pilgrims as part of the deal to fund the enterprise. The Pilgrims, albeit reluctant, did agree to the terms of the contract. Being more accustomed to the feudal laws of the old world, the adventurers pushed this socialist communal idea upon the Pilgrims in last minute negotiations practically as the Pilgrims were about to set sail. The Pilgrims agreed, but again the arrangement was not their preference.

The Pilgrims lived in common houses together, and they worked the common land together. They were to work six days with one day of rest each week. There was no competition because individual merit was neither praised nor rewarded. The fruits of all labor were held in common. All were given the same amount of food at meal times. It was to be a virtual utopia with equal outcomes for everyone. A land of true social justice. A planned and shared society of tranquility and harmony with all workers working equally together for the common good and the general welfare of all.

Under this system of equality of outcome, no matter how hard you worked or how unproductive another man was, everyone received the same amount of the common food supply at meal time. Everyone continued to live in common with the common land and common houses, and all received the same common clothes. Human nature began to reveal itself through this system of forced sharing imposed by the adventurers or investors at the London Company. The Pilgrims became disgruntled, discontent, some were just plane lazy or idle and could hardly be made to work. Keep in mind that these were a good people, by and large, and not a band of criminals or rough cuts. Nevertheless, human nature is the common denominator between all men. And when pressed hard enough even the most

Human nature is the common denominator between all men.

virtuous of men can show their lower nature. The socialist communal arrangement, that contractually obligated the Pilgrims to their agreement with the adventurers of the London Company, also pushed them to the very edge of the dark side of man.

> "The system of common property had occasioned grievous discontents; the influence of law could not compel regular labor like the uniform impulse of personal interest; and even the threat of 'keeping back their bread' could not change the character of the idle."
>
> George Bancroft, *History of the Colonization of the United States*, Vol. I / 1854 [50]

The disruptive and poor attitudes continued and hundreds of Pilgrims died of starvation. Yet the men and women still could not command better of their character since each individual man's labor and effort was bound to the group. Neither law nor whip could goad these men to better behavior under the fixed communal social economic condition in which they found themselves. Merit was not rewarded and the unproductive were given the same as the industrious. The Pilgrims became miserable under these forced *equality of outcome* conditions. No matter how hard one worked it was not allowed to improve one's own plight beyond the most unproductive among them. The socialist system all but destroyed motivation to work even under the looming prospect of starvation and death.

This brought about a period which is called the Starving Time. Have you ever heard of it? You should have been taught of this important part of American history in elementary school. I was not, and you probably weren't either. George Percy, Governor of Jamestown Colony, describes some of this period in the following.

> ...beginning to feel the sharp prick of hunger which no man truly describe but he which hath tasted the bitterness thereof...Then having fed upon horses and other beasts as long as they lasted, we were glad to make shift with vermin as dogs, cats, rats, and mice...[and] to eat boots, shoes, or any other leather some could come by...And now, famine beginning to ghastly and pale in every face, that nothing was spared to maintain life and to do those things which seem incredible- as to dig up dead corpses out of graves and to eat them; and some have licked up the blood which hath fallen from their weak fellows; and amongst the rest, this was most lamentable that one of our colony murdered his wife, ripped the child out of her womb and threw it into the river, and after chopped the mother in pieces and salted her for his food.
>
> George Percy, Governor of Jamestown Colony, 1610 [51]

Keep in mind the Pilgrims could have left and returned to England. They did not because the tyranny of life without freedom and liberty of conscience was even worse than the incredibly dire conditions they now found themselves in. Ponder that for a moment. It's the same frame of mind that the tyranny of George III later drove the American patriots to. It's the reason Patrick Henry declared "give me liberty or give me death." The governor of this group, desirous of improving their lot, wrote the following.

> So they began to think how they might raise as much corn as they could, and obtain a better crop than they had done, that they might not still thus languish in misery...the Governor (with the advice of the chiefest amongst them) gave way that they should set corn every man for his own particular, and in that regard trust to themselves...And so assigned to every family a parcel of land, according to the proportion of their number...This had a very good success, for it made all hands

> very industrious, so as much more corn was planted than otherwise might have been by any means the Governor or any other could use...The women now went willingly into the field, and too their little ones with them to set corn; which before would allege weakness and inability; whom to have compelled would have been thought great tyranny and oppression.
>
> William Bradford, Governor of Plymouth Plantation, 1623, from *Of Plymouth Plantation* [52]

Are you shocked? We are talking about our American Pilgrims and their experiment in socialism. The first economic system implemented here in this land was socialism not capitalism, and it almost sent all of them to their deaths. The Pilgrims did not seek this system. They tried to broker a deal of individual private property with businessman, Thomas Weston, with the London Company, who funded their venture. They were unsuccessful and so they reluctantly accepted the socialist system that was imposed upon them by their financiers. The Christian Pilgrims were well versed in the biblical Scriptures and they knew 2 Thessalonians 3:10 which says, "...if anyone is not willing to work, then he is not to eat, either." The pilgrims believed the application of 2 Thessalonians 3:10 was in accordance with their notion that the unproductive should not live off of the productive. The pilgrims also believed that implementation of this scripture would have improved their plight long ago. Nevertheless, they were contractually committed to fulfilling the terms of the agreement they made—the terms of the socialist economic system the London

Company presented them with just before sailing away on the Mayflower.

Why was this socialistic communal system so destructive to the human character and attitudes of the colonists? After all, we are talking about the Puritans and Pilgrims here. A people that strove extremely hard to live virtuous and moral lives. I think that question was answered in the above information, but I will try to offer a little more light. It is called human nature. Men and things are not the same. Humans are not property. An apple in your hand is pretty much the same as an apple in mine, right? The same is true of most *things* that men need for their lives. But *men* are not the same as *things*. Human beings are individuals and therefore due the respect of their individual humanity. Man is not meant to be cast into a group and have his individuality ignored. Some men are very industrious while others are not. Some men are honest while others tend toward a life of dishonesty. Some men are frugal and plan for the future for themselves and their families, while other men are less frugal and choose to abandon their families. Men are not equal in character or virtue—no man is perfect, but men are not equally imperfect. The comparisons and contrasts could go on and on, but you get the point.

Men are not equal in character or virtue—No man is perfect, but men are not equally imperfect.

People are individual human beings with their own thoughts, feelings, and dreams, and lives. Would you share a common bank account with your hard earned dollars with any ten people you know? Would you share in common a food pantry with ten of your neighbors? What about joint ownership of a house or a car? Would you enter into this type of arrangement with multiple families?

If you answer no, and I call you selfish, as the socialist calls the capitalist, what are your immediate thoughts? I will be the first to say, you are not selfish. Your innate and intuitive knowledge of natural moral law, which all humans have, is likely telling you this group plan will not work. Your intuition is likely telling you it is unwise and destructive of the human spirit to co-mingle the fruits labor into one common pot. Even worse, for that pool of labor to be *forcefully taken by taxation and then redistributed* by a third party, the government and its recipient, who had no part in earning that money. This unjust social redistribution is exactly what socialism does by putting appointed bureaucrats in charge of the distribution of the monies earned by others. This was essentially the economic arrangement of the Pilgrims which was made under the charge of the London Company. This type of government structure is bondage to the human psyche and spirit because men are all different individuals. A government-coerced economic structure is one of the injustices of socialism. Socialism runs contrary to the virtuous aspects of human nature. In other words, intentionally or not, socialism appeals to the baser nature of man because it removes the incentive to be productive. Men's characters, lives, desires, dreams, industriousness, and spirits are simply not to be placed in the same basket with one another as one would a bunch of common apples. A most cruel government structure places individually sovereign human beings into the same common basket or group as if they nothing more than chattel (personal property).

No man has the right to the fruits of another man's labor. Socialism forces man into double bind. First between fellow citizens, and second, with the government. You cannot bind the fate of the productive with the non-productive and expect an outcome of civil societal harmony. When government takes and pools the fruits of divers men's labor, government is also pooling the differing degrees of labor and effort which produced those fruits. Socialism, in effect, pools men's differing characters, their differing value systems, etc. together in a common pool. Binding men's lives together in such a manner is immoral and unjust. This results in turning man against man. It is an injustice against the productive and unjustly rewards the non-productive. Human beings are *individuals* with no two being the same. Socialism is a group philosophy which crushes the individual human spirit. The

Socialism is a group philosophy which crushes the individual human spirit.

economic and human proof of this truth is all around the world, past and present if one would but take a look.

Governor William Bradford further writes the following, (Spelling as written by Bradford).

> The experience that was tried in this comone course and condition, tried sundrie years, and that amongst godly and sober men, may well evince the vanitie of that conceite of Platos & other ancients, applauded by some of later times; that ye taking away of property (private property), and bringing in comunitie into a comone wealth, would make them happy and flourishing; as if they were wiser then God...for ye young men that were most able and fitte for labour & service did repine that they should spend their time & strength to worke for other mens wives and children, without any recompence. The strong, or man of parts, had no more in devission of victails (food) & clothes, then he that was weake and not able to doe a quarter ye other could; this was thought injustice...and for mens wives to be commanded to doe servise for other men, as dressing their meate, washing their clothes, &c., they deemd it a kind of slaverie. Upon ye poynte all being to have alike, and all to doe alike, they thought them selves in ye like condition, and one as good as another, and so, if it did not cut of those relations that God hath set amongest men, yet it did at least much diminish and take of ye mutuall respects that should be preserved amongst them. And would have bene worse if they had been men of another condition. Let none objecte this is men's corruption, and nothing to ye course it selfe. I answer, seeing all men have this corruption in them, God in his wisdom saw another course fiter for them.[53]

Governor Bradford utterly repudiates the socialist system in his own words and in his own writing in his book: *Of Plymouth Plantation 1608-1650*. Socialism almost wiped out all of the Puritan and Pilgrim colonies. Socialism, by its very design, no matter how well-intended, feeds and waters the vices of men. Thus the seed of socialism's appeal is the same seed of its eventual death and man's. Why? Because socialism takes from one man what he has earned and hands to another man what he has not earned. The socialist seeks to call this sharing the wealth. It is not sharing; it is stealing, transferring stolen goods, and causing one citizen to possess stolen goods belonging to another citizen. Socialism is not social justice; Socialism is a system of social injustice. There is no social justice in the act of taking from one and handing to another. This spreads the seeds of bitterness and division between the citizenry. Socialism is a poison to human nature that opens the door to the dark side of man. Socialism does not lift mankind up it, it drives mankind down.

Socialism is not social justice; Socialism is a system of social injustice.

Socialism is not a sustainable system for these reasons. Socialism does not produce for man. It consumes man by destroying individual drive and initiative. The lure of socialism is its emotional appearance of fairness. Politicians have used this deceptive emotional lure for ages to keep themselves in power. This appeal is only emotional and a little thinking and knowledge of history and human nature should lead one to an entirely different place. Sharing is a voluntary act from the human heart, not a forced economic construct through the transfer of one man's labor and efforts to another by government decree. Socialism places man in a kind of stagnated bondage where individually created wealth is consumed by the group at a greater rate than it is created. Therefore, its eventual doom and destructive misery is simply a matter of time. Whereas individual liberty and free market capitalism sets man free and creates abundance. Socialism appeals to the less motivated or inclined and the government bureaucrat regulator because he is in charge via regulation. It will also appeal to people who have been placed in economic duress by government progressives advancing the march of socialism by burdening the economy with excessive regulation.

The socialist bureaucrat increases in power in an almost direct proportion to the number of regulations, rules, and social programs he imposes upon society.

By being in charge of the system the socialist progressive can always appear to be *trying to improve matters.* The socialist bureaucrat increases in power in an almost direct proportion to the number of regulations, rules, and social programs he imposes upon society. The state then grows in power as the individual loses autonomy over his own life.

Fidel Castro tried to improve matters via socialism in Cuba beginning in 1959 when he came to power. He worked on it until his death in November of 2016 while the Cuban people continued to live in privation and political tyranny. His brother, Raúl Castro, is continuing the family tradition of trying to make socialism work while the people suffer. Socialism is the dream of a few men, as they seek legal control and authority over the lives of all the other men. Capitalism is the dream of the individual man as he seeks to live free, in liberty from government bondage while seeking legal authority over no man.

Parents typically have children out of love. Likewise, most parents teach their children in the ways of individual responsibility with the hope of their children eventually living life on their own as productive and happy people. Healthy parents do not have children to have and to hold forever. To allow or aid a child in growing up incompetent and or dependent on others is not love. I ask you, would this not be cruel? Would that be love? To allow a child to become no more than a dependent to you or someone else is not love it is selfishness. What does this teach us about life? What does it teach about capitalism as opposed to socialism? Capitalism relies upon individual initiative and individual liberty to be able to pursue one's dreams. Logically then, if you diminish a man's liberty and take away the fruits of his labor he will not be so inclined to work hard. Why should he? Capitalism is truly the more benevolent system, because it requires individual responsibility and initiative. History makes it clear that socialism is and always has been destructive of man and country alike.

Socialism eventually became an utterly refuted and a hated system by the Pilgrims. Communal living was finally abandoned and private property was instituted by the Pilgrims. Each person or family was given their own plot of several acres to farm. They could now work as individuals, keep what they needed for food and sell or trade the rest for a profit. The productive were no longer ball and chained to the unproductive. Amazingly even the less productive picked up the pace now that they had to work their own gardens.

In1621 they planted 26 acres, in 1622 they planted 60 acres, and in 1623 they had about 184 total acres producing food. Now the Pilgrims had more than they needed and they began to trade with the Indians. Finally, they had abundance and were without want! In 1627 the Pilgrims built a trading post at Aptucxet in Bourne, Massachusetts. It became known as the Aptucxet Trading Post. A reproduction of the Aptucxet Trading Post exists to this day and is built upon the original foundation. Later in 1636 a grist mill was built by Pilgrim John Jenny. John Jenny's grist mill is located in Plymouth Massachusetts. People began to work independently, using their own trades and skill sets. Finally, the blessings of abundance came about. The Pilgrims, after the death and wretched misery of the Starving Time, and after an abundant fall harvest, celebrated their abundance and lack of want by thanking God with the Indians as invited guests. They called it Thanksgiving.

This was the birth of free market capitalism in America. The shackles of old world socialism which bound the unindustrious to the industrious were finally cast off. Each person became free to pursue his or her own interests and to provide a service for a profit.

Mises.org ran an article on Thanksgiving Day November 27, 2014. It said, "Thus the real meaning of Thanksgiving, deleted from the official story, is: Socialism does not work; the one and only source of abundance is free markets..."[54]

America started as a poor nation if measured by material wealth. Would you agree? The Pilgrims had little in material wealth when they arrived. They built everything over time with much cost in anguish, hardship, labor, and death. But they were very rich in the values of natural moral law of nature and strong in faith in nature's God. They were not perfect but they were rich in moral values gleaned from their knowledge of Biblical principles. From these values, instilled into the following generations, America rose from the ground to become the greatest nation and economic power on earth. This is historical fact.

Nevertheless, in 1933 the *Humanist Manifesto* was published. In it the profit motive is condemned. But before we look at it let's consider the following history of life in America before this manifesto of humanism. Consider the Pilgrims plight, struggle, starvation, and death, because of the old world government tyranny and later their contract agreeing to socialism. Consider their eventual blessing of abundance through the liberty of capitalism and individualism rather than communal effort. Recall the bloodshed of the American Revolution and our constitutional individual liberty that came from it. Remember the American industrial revolution which brought us the discovery of oil in

America stands as a tribute to man's belief in nature's God, natural law, constitutional freedom, and free market capitalism.

America and gave us kerosene for lamp light. Then electricity and the light bulb. Andrew Carnegie built a steel bridge over the Mississippi River (a bridge which everyone said was impossible and would collapse) connecting the East Coast with the West Coast via railway. Railways were then built to all parts of America to the point of being overbuilt. Sky-Scrapers began to paint the skylines of our American cities. Henry Ford realizes his dream of building a car that the common man could afford and it was known as the Ford Model A or the A Model. It cost $820.00 dollars. Millions from all parts of the globe were clamoring to get to America for a piece of the action.

Through free market capitalism the greatest and wealthiest middle class the world has ever known became known as the American middle class. America stands as a tribute to man's belief in nature's God, natural law, constitutional freedom, and free market capitalism. Freedom from the presumed authority of the bureaucrat man in government. Free to dream, free to build, free to open a business, free to work and keep all your fruits of labor. Did you know that there was no income tax from America's founding until the big government progressives passed it in 1913. America was free to prosper and prosper America did. And as Americans prospered they began to share their abundance with the world, just as the Pilgrims before them began to trade and share their abundance. All of this and so much more from American free market capitalism and constitutional individual liberty.

Then around 1913 came the red tape of the statist-progressive era of big government. The progressives gave us the IRS, the income tax, and big government social programs, a debased fiat currency along with a massive national debt. A debt that guarantees future taxation to pay it back. Now that America was a wealthy nation statist-progressive politicians wanted control of the mighty economic ship. This was the beginning of the attacks upon the free market capitalist system, and our gold standard which protected the value of the US dollar in your pocket. That free market capitalist system that brought America to this point of world prominence now came under assault by the progressives in the government at the time. This was the beginning of the federal government's wrapping America in the bondage of government over-regulation.

Was America perfect? No, nothing involving man will ever be perfect because man is not perfect. There were still problems and there were still the poor. The problems and the plight of the remaining poor is exactly what the progressive secular humanists focused and seized upon in order to attack American capitalism and American values. The American's historic achievements for themselves and for humankind were overlooked and the focus was kept on the remaining problems. The attack on America was in full swing by the progressives from the inside and outside of government. Thus in 1933 the secular humanists declared, in writing, the following 14th affirmation from their 15 affirmations in their *Humanist Manifesto*.

> The Humanists are firmly convinced that existing acquisitive and profit-motivated society has shown itself to be inadequate and that a radical change in methods, controls, and motives must be instituted. A socialized and cooperative economic order must be established to the end that the equitable distribution of the means of life be possible. The goal of humanism is a free and universal society in which people voluntarily and intelligently cooperate for the common good. Humanists demand a shared life in a shared world.
>
> *Humanist Manifesto*, 1933 [55]

This should clearly show you that no matter the success of free market capitalism and our constitutional freedom, the statist/progressive/socialist will always find a wedge to attempt to shift power from the individual to the state. And there is always a wedge issue available because man is imperfect and therefore anything man creates will be imperfect. These government-first types of people will always find the most emotional and exploitive issues to focus on and demagogue the people into feeling their way toward a false conclusion for yet another reason to grow government. In this case a socialized and cooperative economic order as stated above. Socialism almost destroyed America before she even began. Check out what I am saying for yourself. With the knowledge of the true history in this lesson the humanists' declaration is more than laughable, it is angering to some degree. Why? Because history and present socialist-communist states stand testament to the poverty creating, misery producing, and death system that is collectivism. It should also indicate to you that your freedom and liberty is not paramount to all men. I took years to realize this. I always assumed all men would prefer individual freedom and liberty over government rule. But finally I realized the common man's freedom stands in the way of the statist-progressive men's agenda. They will, for this reason, use deceit, fraud, corruption, government regulation, and fear tactics to diminish your freedom in order to empower the state. You will know them by their fruits. How? The statist progressives almost invariably will use the heightened emotions of any crisis to diminish your freedom and increase the power of the state. For example, a shooter kills someone and the statist's answer is to take your gun. Another example, capitalism does not make everyone equally wealthy. Answer, call it a greed-based and morally corrupt system. Shift power of the purse from the people to the state through socialism. George Bernard Shaw, playwright, said while describing the Fabian Socialist methodology of advancement that

George Bernard Shaw, playwright, said while describing the Fabian Socialist methodology of advancement that they use: "Methods of stealth, intrigue, subversion, and the deception of never calling Socialism by its right name."

they use: "Methods of stealth, intrigue, subversion, and the deception of never calling Socialism by its right name."[56]

Of notable importance the symbol for the Fabian Socialist Society is the wolf in sheep's clothing. You can easily find this on the Internet with a simple image search. You should have a look, I think.

The antidote to all this illogic, vice and deception is critical thinking, self education, knowledge of history, virtuous living, solid moral values, and faith in natures God. Know what you think, and most importantly, know why you think what you think.

At the outset I asked a question—What is capitalism and what is its driving force? Is it greed or something else. The common attack upon capitalism is that it is a greed-based system that exploits people and results in a few winners. Let's have a closer look.

So what is capitalism? Capitalism is a voluntary system of individuals trading their privately owned property in mutually beneficial exchanges. That's it, nothing untoward here at all. People owning private property and trading their own property just like the Pilgrims and the Aptucxet Trading Post. You see capitalism is about you trading your stuff. You don't need the government for that. Socialism is about the government wedging itself into the middleman position in order to regulate and control the trading of your stuff and then by taxing you and taking your money for their political desires. This is why the socialist, to gain governmental power, is forever regulating and criticizing capitalism. Here is the dirty little secret. The socialist needs the capitalist's money, but the capitalist does not need the socialist. Capitalism is a sustainable system because it produces wealth, operates privately and independently from government as individuals trade their own things. Socialism, and its end stage, Communism, is an unsustainable system because it consumes wealth and grows government to unsustainable levels. Also, it must be involuntarily managed and controlled by force of law via government. Capitalism empowers the individual over his or her life while socialism empowers the state and its bureaucrats over you and your own life.

Consider the following quotes from the Communist Manifesto:

> "We communists have been reproached with the desire of abolishing the right of personally acquiring property as the fruit of a man's own labor, which property is alleged to be the groundwork of all personal freedom, activity, and independence..."
>
> "....The Communists are further reproached with desiring to abolish countries and nationality..."
>
> "....communism abolishes eternal truths, it abolishes all religion, and all morality..."
>
> "Abolition of the family!"
>
> the "...abolition of individuality and freedom! And rightly so..."
>
> "....that by "individual" you mean no other person than the bourgeois, than the middle-class owner of property. This person must, indeed, be swept out of the way, and made impossible..."
>
> "....on capital, on private gain..."
>
> "A heavy or progressive graduated income tax."[57]

Now consider the following from President Johnson's progressive or socialist Great Society Speech in 1964 at the University of Michigan Commencement: "For a century we labored to settle and to subdue a continent. For half a century we called upon unbounded (unregulated) invention and untiring industry to create an order of plenty for all our people."[58]

In his own speech President Johnson in 1964 admits that free market capitalism inspires an untiring human spirit, "unbounded invention and untiring industry."[59] This untiring human liberty motivated the people to, "create an order of plenty for all our people."[60] He then, essentially says, we should use the wealth created by capitalism to transform into a socialist country. What?

Then he continues: "The challenge of the next half century is whether we have the wisdom to use that wealth to enrich and elevate our national life, and to advance the quality of our American civilization."[61]

What? President Johnson, in 1964, advocated taking privately earned and owned fruits of labor and redistributing it nationally—*socialism*. Moreover, he asks if we have the *wisdom* to do this. What? After the history lesson America gave the world in human liberty and freedom? After America's meteoric rise to the world stage, he advocates a turn to socialism. The full speech is online and well worth reading.

The period I have just described from 1913 until President Johnson's great speech in 1964, and forward to the present has largely been politically and economically dominated by progressive statist big government growth and regulation. Thus, the total number of years America has now been under big government regulation and expansion is now approximately 103 years. From the founding (1791, the year our Constitution was ratified) until the progressive era began in approximately 1913 was about 122 years. By President Johnson's own admission America spent approximately the first half of its existence creating liberty and prosperity. He then proclaims we now need socialist redistribution to share that wealth to the nation. In my opinion, this move toward progressive socialism for the past 103 years of American history is the reason we are now in such economic turmoil and national debt. What is your view?

A radio broadcaster, back in 1965, made a famous broadcast. Keep in mind 1965 was 52 years after the progressive era began in earnest around 1913. In that 1965 radio address by Paul Harvey entitled "Freedom to Chains," he warns America not to follow in the footsteps of the fall of Rome due to moral corruption, highly-regulated and bloated government, and currency devaluation, the famous Paul Harvey stated the following:

> They bore bountiful fruit, and when they bore bountiful fruit the people got fat, and when they got fat they got lazy, and when they got lazy they began to want to absolve themselves of personal responsibility and began to turn over to government to do for them things which traditionally they had been doing for themselves. At first there appears to be nothing wrong asking government to perform some extra service for you. But if you ask government for extra services government in order to perform its increasing function has to

> get bigger, right? And as government gets bigger in order to support its increasing size it has to what? Tax the individual more. So the individual gets littler, and to collect the increased taxes requires more tax collectors, so the government gets bigger, in order to pay the individual tax collector, it has to tax the individual more so the government gets bigger and the individual gets littler and the government gets bigger and the individual gets littler until the government is all powerful and the individual is hardly anything at all. The government is all powerful and the people are cattle...You know they even had a transportation act back there prescribing the fee required to rent one laden ass per mile...which meant in order to make Ta profit a jackass would have to carry 5 passengers....it was simply beyond the capacity of the jackass...and Rome passed into what history has recalled as the dark ages lasting a thousand years...
>
> Paul Harvey, *Freedom to Chains*, 1965 [62]

The push of America to a socialist nation is not new here folks. The progressives' fundamental transformation of America to a socialist state has had many decades now to grow destructive bureaucratic regulatory weeds throughout our system and we must become informed and awake now.

Is the driving force of capitalism greed as the socialist says? Capitalism is simply an economic system. In other words, it is an economic tool. Put the tool of capitalism in the hands of a group of generally corrupt individuals full of vice and you will have one result in the type of transactions that take place. Greed and product quality corruption will likely be present in this scenario. Put the tool of capitalism in the hands of a generally virtuous and moral group of individuals and you will have quite a different result. Quality products made with pride, integrity, and generally honest transactions will dominate this scenario. Capitalism is a tool and the products of that tool depend entirely upon the hand the tool is placed in. Therefore, the blanket charge of greed as the driving force is clearly not the case. It depends upon the people employing the tool. And this is why morality matters.

Early in America's history the people were a largely honest, moral, and virtuous lot and America's capitalistic abundance is testament to that truth. Now this is not a Pollyanna statement with the delusion that America was perfect nor ever will be. People are imperfect so the systems people create will also be imperfect. To go down this road is to miss the point. The point is that free market capitalism, the kind we Americans speak of, is a system that serves and uplifts man, but it needs a healthy moral base to be placed upon in order to be honest, productive, and to keep corruption at bay. I fully think and believe that America's economic decline can be directly correlated to her increase in big government socialized red-tape bureaucracy, beginning around 1913, and due to the moral thus cultural decline of her people.

People are imperfect so the systems people create will also be imperfect.

If you recall the statement made by George Bernard Shaw that the socialist method is to employ deceit when advancing socialism. Do you not think that it is to the socialist's advantage to attempt to frustrate and harm the workings of individual liberty and of capitalism by heavy regulation, cultural decline, class divisions, and other means in order to bring about a socialist state in

American capitalism must be freed from the shackles of progressive big government regulation in order to bring our economy back and to lift the burden of government from her people.

America? George Bernard Shaw said to never call socialism by its rightful name. So they speak of *regulation* instead of socialism. I certainly think so and I think the history and data back up this notion. The statist progressives in America have been heavily regulating our capitalistic system for over one hundred years now. It's a wonder that we have an economy at all. This must change and we must return to true free market capitalism. American capitalism must be freed from the shackles of progressive big government regulation in order to bring our economy back and to lift the burden of government from her people.

Capitalism of the sort most Americans think of when they think or speak of capitalism requires a generally honest and moral people and likewise an honest, moral, and just government. This is one reason why morality is integral to the success of our country on all levels.

The tool of capitalism firmly built upon a moral and ethical foundation is based upon service not greed. Greed is the motivation of the scam artist not the capitalist. Good service and a quality product is the motivation of the moral capitalist. Good service and quality products are not the fruits of the greedy man.

The greedy man is after the quickest dollar possible and is not looking to build solid long-term business relationships between himself and his customer base.

> *Profit is the harvest of labor and investment.*

The capitalist knows if he is to succeed he must first provide a quality product or service at an affordable price. Therefore, service comes before profit. And if there be poor service there will likely be low profit. Capitalism, unlike socialism, calls a man to his virtues by taking pride in producing a quality product or service that he is proud to claim and one that his customer is proud to own. Many capitalists may work for months or years and invest thousands, or hundreds of thousands, or even millions of dollars, before ever seeing a single dollar as profit. This is not greed, it is the spirit of service, and the pride of quality products, in hopes for a return on investment or profit at some distant future date. Simply because a man makes a profit does not make him greedy. Does the laborer make a profit? Yes, it's his pay check for his time and service. Profit is the harvest of labor and investment. Whether it be the business owner or the hired worker.

Free Market Distribution of Wealth

The free market capitalist system is an unbiased, objective, and socially just distributor of wealth throughout an economy. Everyone that participates gets a piece of the pie. The following is an example of the basic functions and products of free market capitalism. We'll call our example "Free Market U.S.A."

In Free Market U.S.A.,

- The shoe cobbler makes and sells quality shoes so he makes a profit.
- With some of this profit he pays his employees their labor profit and they each go buy groceries.
- The grocer runs a quality store and his customers are happy so he makes a profit.
- With this profit he pays his employees their labor profit and they all buy new cars.
- The car manufacture makes a great car and has happy customers so he makes a profit.
- With this profit he pays his employees their labor profit, and they each go buy a new house.
- The home builder makes a solid house and has happy customers so he makes a profit also.
- With this profit he pays his employees their labor profit and they all go to buy new clothes.
- The tailor sells new clothes to his customers but, uh, something is wrong. His customers are all complaining of inferior quality and bad fitting. The free market regulation via customers says good bye to him and he is out of business. He loses his business investment and his employees are now out of a job.

- A new tailor, one of the employees of the prior tailor, has been saving his money and can now invest in his own shop. He opens for business and hires the employees that are looking for a job.

This scenario replicates itself throughout our country and that is basic to how a free market economy works, regulates itself, and spreads the wealth. All who participate in the capitalist system gain from the capitalist system. To each producer according to his investment in money, time, and labor; from each consumer according his free market need or desire to purchase. It is really quite simple and easy to understand. The poor quality products get exposed and expunged by the free market consumer regulator without the need of a government regulator.

To each producer according to his investment in money, time, and labor; from each consumer according his free market need or desire to purchase.

Now, consider the impact of government regulation and taxation to each of the above businesses. Enforcing the regulations cost time and money, therefore, the owner would have to make up this loss somewhere. The regulatory and tax cost would likely show up in lost jobs and higher prices. The point to understand is that government regulation and taxation cost you the consumer. We all pay the price for the regulators and their regulations. A few basic rules in the free market are all that is needed. But if regulation is

Overregulation is death to capitalism but birth to socialism.

not monitored and kept to a minimum it overburdens the system. The economy then becomes bound, gagged, and controlled by the regulatory agencies, as it currently is.

The example also shows how an employee can save his profits and eventually open a business of his own. There is economic mobility in a free market for those willing to be responsible and frugal enough to save and build capital for an investment of their own. The example shows how free market capitalism benefits everyone that participates in the economy. Government overregulation can actually keep some from participating, cost jobs, and increase prices. The government has a role, but it is minimal. Its encroachment beyond the minimally necessary negatively impacts our economy. Overregulation is death to capitalism but birth to socialism.

All markets have natural cycles due to technological advancement, etc. For example, the horse and buggy industry lost to the automobile industry but society and the consumer benefited. Therefore, there will be, from time to time, loss of businesses and jobs like the example of the tailor above. But the free market will absorb and correct these problems quickly and efficiently if left alone to do so. The consumer is the free market regulatory agent. American free market capitalism has created the greatest middle class the world has ever known, and the strongest and most economically powerful nation the world has ever known.

Socialism is a system of deceptive false benevolence. It is spoken of as a way to distribute wealth to the poor which has an emotionally appealing ring to it. We all care about the poor but taking the fruits of one man's labor and handing it to another man is neither moral, sharing, nor benevolent. Socialism has no credible rational or moral basis whatsoever. It enslaves men as we have seen. It also empowers the bureaucrat politician through its system of mummifying regulatory red tape. It threatens the autonomy of the individual citizen and his private property. The socialist makes the charge of greed to the capitalist. But I ask you, who is the greedy? The man who earns or the man who takes? Socialism is built of greed and false benevolence. The American citizen free market capitalist has always given to charity out of his free market abundance. The socialist claims to want fairness, equality, and social justice. But fairness, equality, and justice cannot be achieved through the injustice of a system that takes from one and hands to the other. A vice cannot produce a virtue and taking fruit from the hand of labor is a vice. Equality of outcome is not a natural state of man and it would be quite an unnatural state of existence for man.

...fairness, equality, and justice cannot be achieved through the injustice of a system that takes from one and hands to the other.

Equality of man would require government force and moral injustice to sustain it and that is not liberty, it is bondage. Nature's morality does not seek equality it seeks moral justice, and moral justice is achieved when the moral laws of nature are left un-manipulated. Likewise, economic justice and balance is achieved when each man is free to enjoy the fruits of his own labor according to his own effort and time.

Capitalism on the other hand requires men to serve one another if they are to succeed. Your services and products must be of good quality and acceptable to the consumer. If not, capitalism will naturally regulate (at no cost to the consumer and with no need of a bureaucrat) or weed out the scam artist and the void will be filled readily by the free market. Capitalism calls upon the responsibility of man and his virtues if he is to succeed. It is difficult to fire a poor performer in a bureaucracy but in the real world poor performance is not tolerated at all by the free market. The inefficient, unproductive, and poor quality products are quickly weeded out. These people will return with a better attitude toward work if the socialist would stop the handouts. Logically, then, capitalism calls upon man to do his best in order to succeed. Socialism is like the bad parent who creates dependents and bondage of its citizens. Socialism brings out the worst in mankind as history, and Venezuela have shown. Capitalism is like the good parent that requires individual responsibility that results in independence and freedom for all who are willing to participate.

Even the most unproductive among us will not stand forever in the fire of poverty if we cease handing him logs.

The Takeaway for Freedom's Defense: Capitalism rewards initiative by requiring service before profit. While Socialism rewards lack of initiative by handing out profit before the requirement of service.

Chapter 8

The Minimum Wage

The Assault on Freedom: Minimum wage regulation is price fixing. Price fixing costs minimum wage jobs, and increases product prices.

The basic of the basics of economics that you must know is that economies are about products and numbers. The products are a service or a thing people want. The numbers are money people want. Free market capitalism is simply people trading things they want for dollars they also want. Doesn't sound so evil, does it? This is the basis of what an economy is. The seemingly hard to understand complexities of economics are more about the complex trade deals that some people make between themselves than it is about economics. If I want to sell you a No. 2 pencil for $50, I am quite certain you will say no. If I say okay, what about 10 cents? You will likely say "deal" if you want the pencil. This free market transaction reveals another simple fact about free market economics called "Price Discovery." Price discovery in this example came about through the free market negotiation for the pencil. I couldn't get you to pay $50 for my pencil, so I lowered my price to a price that you, as my customer, would pay. Together we discovered the market price through fair negotiation. The market price for the no. 2 pencil was established at (10 cents). One last item. This free market trade is based on my being able to make the pencil for less than 10 cents. This is obviously true because I cannot stay in business if I can't sell my pencil for a little more than it cost me to make. Also, the more it cost to make, the more you will have to pay.

Fact # 1

No number (cost or expense) in a free market economy is arbitrary. All numbers in a free market absent governments massive regulations were arrived at by price discovery. Government intervention in free market capitalism distorts price discovery. All the numbers have a "raison d'être," or a reason to be the number that it is.

Fact # 2

Each number (cost or expense) is part of a link or chain of numbers. Remember, no number is arbitrary and no number stands alone. So, if you change one number, another number must change also. Example: to make my pencil I have to pay manufacturing costs such as my employees, building rent, pencil materials like wood, packaging, advertising, government regulation, etc. All these things have a number which is a cost to me as the manufacturer (price discovery). Now, if one or more of the costs goes up, I have to increase the cost of my pencils. If the cost increase is more than my customers will pay, then I have to cut my cost to make the pencil. If I can do neither, I will go out of business because I will be losing money. If I go out of business this is bad for the customer also.

Product competition is the hero to the consumer in a free market economy because it drives down prices as it increases product quality.

Why? Because now there is less competition in the pencil business. If there were no competition a pencil maker could get a high non-market-discovered price for his pencil. Competition is part of price discovery and competition is the friend of the customer or consumer because it helps to lower cost and increase the value of the product. Product competition is the hero to the consumer in a free market economy because it drives down prices as it increases product quality.

Fact # 3

There are two principle numbers that all business must be concerned with.

A. The COST to make a product or service.

B. The market selling PRICE of that product or service.

Fact # 4

If cost increases (one or more of the numbers in the chain goes up), then selling price must increase.

If price discovery will not allow for the price increase (customer refuses to pay the increased price) then the pencil maker must cut cost. The easiest way to cut cost is? You guessed it—one or more employees will get fired.

Fact # 5

Profit is good for the business owner and you. Profit means that the owner can keep running his business and it means that you get to keep your job and profit from your labor.

If No profit... No business... No jobs

All of the previous material is intended to help you understand that economies are dynamic. Economies are, in an economic sense, alive. They respond to all sorts of stimuli that affect cost and profit, and they are very sensitive to these stimuli. An economy has billions of economic chain reactions (response to stimuli) going on every moment of the day and night throughout the world. This is why you see prices going up at times (most times it seems) as cost increases, and sometimes prices go down as cost decreases or competition increases. Markets are alive so you can't just poke at them with a stick. Government regulation is a stick that pokes at markets all the time. The customer and employee don't typically see the government poking stick (of regulation) but the business owner does. The customer sees the price go up and directs his frustration at the business. He gets mad at the insurance company, gas company, grocer, doctor, etc.

What he doesn't see is the government poking regulations at the business owners forcing them to comply with these costly and time consuming regulations, which increase cost thereby prices, as we just learned.

I hope you are beginning to understand why the government arbitrarily picking a number to increase the minimum wage is that poking stick. If the government takes this action, as it has done so many times in the past, jobs will be lost just as in the past. This is a fact and has been proven over and over. The difficulty here is that the government often appears to be trying to help the poor or people employed at minimum wage, when it in fact harms them. An additional point concerning government. Why is it that you never hear the government suggesting that it could cut taxes for minimum wage earners, if it truly wanted to help? What if the government just eliminated income taxes for minimum wage earners altogether. The government could effectively increase the minimum wage by cutting the income tax or eliminating it for minimum wage workers. Why is that never suggested? It is almost as if they hope you don't notice this idea is always missing from the discussion. The government could also cut regulation on the business owner and that would in turn help the employee.

Consider the following conversation between two friends; Jack and Jill.

Jack: "Hey, why don't you buy that car that you were looking at? It's obvious you like it."

Jill: “I want to but I don’t have enough money.”

Jack: “Just go get more money!”

Jill: Dumfounded at Jack’s basic lack of knowledge of economics, but kindly replies, “That’s not how life works, Jack.”

The above may seem silly in its format, but it makes a clean point of the matter.

Surely by now the facts are clear. Jill can’t simply run to the money tree for the additional money for the car she wants any more than the business owner can run to the money tree for the government poking it with the regulation stick of a mandated minimum wage increase. This will cause some to lose their jobs, period.

“If a man is paying you five dollars an hour, you give him ten dollars in effort. That’s how you get ahead.”

A Novel Idea to Consider

As an employee, consider this idea that my father once taught me. You add value to yourself and the service you are providing by first helping the business owner increase his profit. I can almost hear my dad now, “If a man is paying you five dollars an hour, you give him ten dollars in effort. That’s how you get ahead.”

Consumers seek price value and product quality. Business owners seek consumers (customers). Thus the business owner who provides the best nexus or combination between price value and product quality will have the most customers, thus profit over time. Why not help him to provide the best quality he can.

In much the same way, employers seek value and quality in their employees. Employees seek money. So consider that the employee who offers the employer the greatest value and quality of service in his labor and effort will thereby command the maximum wage per hour. Thus wages are determined by value. Remember that price discovery mechanism we talked about? Why not apply it to yourself and increasing your own value by being the best you can be and offering that best self as a service to the market.

So take my Dad's advice. Give twice what you are paid for. That is how you get ahead.

The Takeaway for Freedom's Defense: The free market will serve the consumer, but the regulated market must serve the government.

Chapter 9

No Right of Provision

The Assault on Freedom: A government that provides the fruit for one man's table by taking it from another man's table is guilty of theft.

Rights. What are rights and where do they come from? Do people have different rights, or are rights all the same for each individual? Do groups have rights or only individuals? Does a king or government have the authority over your rights, thereby having the power to alter, enhance, or remove them? Or do you and your rights have authority independent the king or government? If you do have rights do these rights innately or by nature carry with them any obligation to others?

As an intellectual exercise look at the list below and determine if you think the item is a right or not. You may want to use a pen and mark each one for later reference. Which of the following items are rights:

Food	Water
Free Speech	Right of conscience of religion or belief
Housing	The internet
Education	Medical care
Driving a car	Paid Pregnancy leave from work
A job	Minimum wage
Cell phone	Welfare support
Owning a gun	Unemployment compensation
Paid vacation	Group rights
Not be offended	

There are other items that could make the list but I think this is sufficient for our purpose.

In determining and assessing what rights are and their origin, all of the afore mentioned questions appear to be valid questions that must be answered. In that vein, let's consider first what a right is by offering a definition and explanation of what a right is not.

A right cannot be anything that denies the right of another person and a right is derived from nature and nature's God.

A right cannot be anything that denies the right of another person and a right is derived from nature and nature's God.

A right, therefore, cannot serve one person while making the other person his servant. Let's take food from the previous list for example. Consider this conversation from two very different people, namely Karl and George.

Karl says, "I have a right to have food."

George, "No you do not. If you have a right to food, then who will you appoint to provide it for you?"

Karl replies, "The government should provide my food."

George then says, "The government has no money to buy food unless it takes the money from the people by taxes or if it prints the money creating debt for the people. Either way the people are paying for your food. Karl, by what authority can you demand the people to buy your food?"

"Because of my humanity I have a human right to food," Karl says.

George answers, "If everyone at the same time, in their humanity, demands his human right to food, who then should be compelled to supply the food? In other words, Karl, who should be made to serve the needs of the other and by what authority do you presume to have to order and position people in this manner. Moreover, are you not denying or encroaching upon the freedom of some while granting unearned or unmerited benefits to others? Benefits that you ask the government take by force of law from another equal citizen?"

Karl, obviously frustrated and having no answer, lashes out at George. "You are a cold-hearted hater of humanity. You don't care if all the people have food or not."

George replied, "Oh no. Demanding the government to provide food for some by the labor of another is an encroachment upon the freedom of the producers or providers of the food while meriting the recipients with food they did not earn. The government subjugation of one citizen to the service of another citizen is destructive to society. This sows the seeds of dissent, division, envy, and general societal destruction. It denies individual rights or freedom of some in favor of others. A right cannot be anything that denies the right of another."

George thought a minute then continued. "You have no right of provision. No one owes you anything but to respect your individual rights as you respect the individual rights of others. But you are free to pursue your happiness on your own and provide for your own food. In this way the freedom of all the people is preserved without encroaching or trampling upon the rights of anyone."

The government subjugation of one citizen to the service of another citizen is destructive to society.

Karl, still refusing to admit to the conflicting nature of his argument, caused George to scratch his head and ponder Karl's motive. Karl seemed to George more intent and interested upon the forcing and arranging people into specific roles in society than actually feeding them. George made this conclusion because Karl simply wouldn't agree to allow the people to each seek their own food.

What could possibly be wrong with this? thought George. This way maximizes freedom of all and denies the rights of none.

> *Government has no inherent or natural right over man, but man has an inherent natural right over government.*

All men being equal in their humanity each have the same exact individual and privately held rights. All humans are born with inherent natural rights. The right to speak, believe in what you wish, act in a manner according to your beliefs, to defend yourself, to pursue your own happiness in whatever way that you choose and so on. Government has no inherent or natural right over man, but man has an inherent natural right over government. Man creates government—government does not create man. Man precedes government, therefore, man's rights precede government. Government has no authority over man except that which is freely given by consent from the man to the government. Man has every right to create or dissolve any government as the governed may choose.

The Cato Institute's Pocket Constitution states, "We are all created equal, as defined by our natural rights; thus, no one has rights superior to those of anyone else. Moreover, we are born with those rights, we do not get them from government—indeed, whatever rights or powers government has come from us, from 'the Consent of the Governed.'"[63]

A man alone in the state of nature, for example, who seeks to howl at the moon each night at 3 a.m. is free to do so in a state of nature away from civil society. But man seeking to live in civil society together with other men agrees to suspend that right in order to live peaceably among others in a civil society. It is important to note that the government does not take the right to howl away from the man because that right is not the government's to take. It is critical to grasp this point at its depth. Your rights are entirely yours. The right belongs to the man and he freely and voluntarily suspends it in order to live in society and thus respect the others' right to a quiet silent night. The right to howl has not been given up, just voluntarily suspended. If the man returns to his state of nature surrounded by acres of his land, he is certainly free to continue once again his right to howl at the moon.

Your rights are a part of you just as your arms, legs, eyes, ears, or your brain. As a human being you have every right to exist and live without being subjugated by the government to serve another citizen. But remember, you must also give the same respect to others and their rights. Whether you agree with another's personal views or not, is of no consequence. No matter your beliefs, lifestyle, your likes, or dislikes. No human has any innate authority over any other human. Authority over man belongs to nature's God and any man who claims otherwise is thereby interjecting himself between man and God which the statist (kings, queens, dictators, tyrants, progressives) has done time and time again throughout history.

For the atheist, by way of illustration, one may ask who could stand between his individual rights and God? He has no belief in

God? No, as is his right to this choice, but all men's rights come from nature and all are equal in these rights and no man, thus, stands between the atheist and his natural rights. By the same measure, you are not owed anything by any other man. Again, you have no right of provision. No human has a right to place, by legal compulsion, any other human to provide for him. Therefore, you have no right to provision of education, food, housing, medical care, internet, etc. because you have no right to compel another person to provide these things to or for you. You cannot claim your humanity or your human rights as your basis to have government take from one and give to you. This is true even if you or others think or feel this thing to be critical to human survival. Food for instance. You cannot claim your "humanity" as a basis for desiring that the government provide food to you. Food that another person must pay for. What about the other guy and his individual rights that you are thereby trampling? No one must be made by law to labor and provide for the other, but all must be protected by government to be free to labor and provide for themselves.

No one must be made by law to labor and provide for the other, but all must be protected by government to be free to labor and provide for themselves.

Caring for those in need is a moral issue for individuals and private institutions like churches, synagogues, civic organizations, and the many other independent private charity organizations that our country is so blessed with. The needs of the poor must be attended to, and people of any just moral society should care for the needy in this way. This moral caring, for lack of a better phrase, is no role for the government. The government is we, is it not? What is to be said then if we as the people pass the plate of charity to be filled by the unnamed bureaucrat instead of ourselves. Can we then say we are a charitable people? Charity is an individual act of the heart. This does not preclude a group, a church or local civic organization for example, from acting from the heart. It does, however, remove it from the bureaucrat.

Please consider the following. A bureaucrat takes money from a citizen he does not know and the citizen has no idea where his money is going. That citizen may very well need the money to feed his own family. Nevertheless, the bureaucrat takes his money and sends it via check to an unknown recipient, the recipient gets the money in the mailbox but thanks no one, because there is no one there to thank. In time this apparent government benevolence has a tendency to breed attitudes of entitlement, at least in many. The recipient, in time, is deceived into thinking that the government has its own money and is charitable, when in reality the government took the money from someone else. Should I take your wallet and buy food for the homeless man on the corner? Shall I then declare myself a good person and take credit for being charitable?

Charity is the role of the private sector. We as a people have done ourselves a great disservice by allowing the government to place itself in the role of the great pretender of charity. The money that the government gives away in its own name comes from us. This has been going on for so long now that far too many people actually think that it's the government's money.

By contrast when individuals or private groups commit to acts of charity there is human contact, there are smiles or tears of thankfulness, hugs and handshakes, attitudes of gratefulness are engendered upon both the recipient and the giver. This is where humanity should rightfully again take up its role of charity, on the local level, human to human where humanity meets humanity. If we do this, we will all benefit greatly. Moreover, the local community knows the homeless man on the corner, not the bureaucrat a thousand miles away. There are many institutions that are and have been doing this for many years and they are to be commended. I am speaking, however, of reclaiming the role that we the people have abdicated to the federal government.

The money that the government gives away in its own name comes from us.

I emphasize these points because the Karls of the world always seem to point to the poor as support for their claim that government must play the role of the provider of certain human rights. Governments have used the pretext of charity to obtain votes and keep certain people in power for decades. The government taking from one and pretending to be the charitable giver to another is a form of theft not charity. Charity is important, but it is not the role of the federal government to choose to whom it will give to and whom it will take from. Charity is the role of the people. We the people, as America has always shown, can establish private local and private national means of filling this role beyond what already exists, if necessary. I am only making the point that the government playing the pretender is immoral in its practice of taking from one and handing out to another. All wrapped in a pretty blanket of government pretense of charity, while it is fully corrupt in its methods and bureaucracy. The only legitimate role of government is to secure the individual rights for each of us.

The government taking from one and pretending to be the charitable giver to another is a form of theft not charity.

In a Letter to M. Divernois, 1795, Thomas Jefferson wrote, "It is to secure these rights that we resort to government at all."[64]

Constitutional government is created by man to protect our rights from one another and to protect our rights from the government itself. You are free, however, to compensate anyone to provide a product or service on your behalf. You are also free to give to anyone and any charity. Why then must government play the middle-man? I think the answer is obvious. Any government claim to benevolence is refuted by its act of taking from one and handing to another. This is wrong and creates division and discontent among the people. Any people or government that seeks to employ one part of the citizenry to the service or support of another part of the citizenry is acting beyond the authority of the constitution. The constitution being the supreme law of the land, one can correctly say that these individuals in government are acting in an unconstitutional and lawless manner, regardless of whether they have managed to pass laws to the contrary. A threat to one man's rights is a threat to all men's rights.

Any breach in freedom's principle wall,
is a threat to the rights of one and all,
and so united on principle we must stand
or divided without principle we shall fall.

Many in the politically correct camp attempt to claim a right not to be offended. Our constitution clearly states that all men have the right to freedom of speech. Nowhere is there any right not to be offended. In fact, the whole reason to have the right of free speech is because men do not agree upon all things said therefore speech gets legal protection. There cannot be the right of free speech and a right not to be offended. The two are mutually exclusive. Any speech can be said to offend the sensibilities of someone, which is why free speech is codified or written into our law. Moreover, if there were a right not to be offended this presumed right would have the effect of shutting down some people's voices because they are said to be offensive. The very notion of being offended is a direct assault upon the principle of free speech. In my study of

Questions are to truth as fire is to gold because in each, through each, their purity is revealed.

this issue it seems clear to me this is the goal of the politically correct movement, just as it was used by tyrants of the past to shut down the voice of dissent. It is part of the cultural Marxist movement. Many Americans have fallen prey to this because, I think, Americans are a generally kind lot and do not wish to go around offending people. In the past common etiquette coupled with generally good basic morals, typically assured citizens had mutual respect for one another. Perhaps we, as a culture, will once again regain our composure in these matters and be respectful of one another's opinions. One is an impostor as to its claim of being a right. Being offended is a false claim, a trumped up fallacy of emotion to go after the principle of free speech. I am quite sure the tyrant is offended by cries for freedom and open discourse because it threatens his rule. It is the lie that seeks the shadow of protection by its bearers, and that very shadow is the denial of open discourse. Truth loves questions, while the lie cowers in fear of even the hint of one. History proves the point beyond doubt.

There is one other very important point to make concerning freedom of speech. Questions are to truth as fire is to gold because in each, through each, their purity is revealed. Freedom of speech is critical to the advancement and integrity of all matters involving man from religion, government, to science. Freedom of speech is the friend of truth and, therefore, freedom. Thomas Paine said, "He who dares not offend cannot be honest."[65]

For this discussion on rights I selected three false rights, from the list at the beginning of this chapter to use as examples. These are the false rights being used to attack the principle of individual rights. These false rights are, 1. food, 2. not to be offended, and 3. group rights. These three best make the points I have tried to convey on this topic. Their examples will make full display of their inherent dangers to freedom and its companion, individual rights. The list contains many more and you can think through each of them yourself. You may find it interesting to do this and compare your final list to your beginning list.

You will find examples throughout this book that show how our fundamental founding principles of freedom are being assaulted and subverted. There is an assault, an attempt at fundamental transformation of our country, taking place on the level of principle but with the appearance of it taking place on the level of the innocuous, superficial, or insignificant issue. The seemingly benign or insignificant issue is thus used to attack the principle while simultaneously acting as a decoy to disguise the seriousness of the attack upon the founding principle. There truly is a fundamental attempt at transforming our nation and shifting power from the individual rights of each and every one of us to the government. The notion of group rights is yet another attempt at this subversive sleight of the intellectual hand.

I previously tried to explain how being offended is used to assault free speech at the fundamental principle level. The notion of group rights employs much the same mechanisms and deceptive methodology in its assault upon individual rights.

The group rights Marxist scheme is explained in the following: A group is considered and chosen to be the recipient of special group rights. There are many contemporary examples of this but I have selected a situation from our American past that best exemplifies the issue, and avoids unwarranted contemporaneous emotional interference or influence. This way makes a clean and clear point of the assault tactic of group rights and its inherent dangers and direct assault on individual rights.

Individual rights and group rights cannot co-exist. Individual rights protect individual citizens and none are left out. Group rights conflict with individual rights. It may seem counter-intuitive that group rights do not protect everyone in society, but they do not as the following will clearly show. Individual rights do protect the individual and his rights and it is the only mechanism that does. Your individual rights are your barrier of protection against a government or any person desiring to abridge or breach your rights, thus, your freedom. Moreover, you must protect the same individual rights of others in order preserve the individual rights for yourself. This is precisely why our founders placed the focus on the individual and not on group rights.

I offer for the claim above the following example: Prohibition! The period in which the sale of alcohol was made illegal in the U.S. The protected group or class in this case was the society at large. The assaulted class of individuals were those who were drinking too much according to the government. The United States government decided that for the greater good of society the individuals who were drinking excessively should be made to stop drinking. In this case the government sided with the group of Americans who believed there should be no drinking. The government trampled the individual rights of one group of Americans, the drinkers so to speak, and favored another group, the non-drinkers or prohibitionists. A decision based on the notion of the greater good, the Marxist notion that the end result justifies the method.

America had a drinking problem, according to the U.S. government in the 1920s, and the progressives believed that the greater good would be to stop the drinking no matter how the goal would be achieved. The government unconstitutionally shifted its duty from the protection the individual rights of all to the protection of a particular favored group. This axiomatically denied the rights of the individual. It is critical to understand the distinction here. For the greater good of the society, some citizens were denied their individual rights and the consequences were deadly and criminal. Excessive drinking certainly has its problems, but the sword of the law to enforce a Marxist group solution is

Marxist not American. The government used a Marxist approach of force, while trampling the citizens' individual rights and worse, in this case.

The United States government and many United States citizens zealously forced their opinion upon the people they disagreed with and resorted to killing the people they disagreed with in order to have their way.

The United States government and many United States citizens zealously forced their opinion upon the people they disagreed with and resorted to killing the people they disagreed with in order to have their way. The United States Government actually poisoned the alcohol knowing full well this would likely result in the deaths of many. It did just that. Estimates on the low end have the number at 10,000 deaths and on the upper end it is somewhere around 50,000 deaths caused by the intentional poisoning of the alcohol. This is one of the best examples that explains the inherent dangers of group rights and how group rights destroy the rights of the individual. This concept may seem illusive at first thought, but I encourage you to ponder it for a while. Group rights are an assault on our individual rights. Individual rights protect all U.S. citizens under the same equal protection. This example should make this point very clear. This is why our founders gave us the notion of individual rights. To protect you, as an individual from anyone who wishes you harm even if it be the government itself. Group rights and individual rights are mutually exclusive—one is Marxist based and controls men in groups and the other is liberty based and frees men as individuals. The group rights movement is a fundamental assault on the principle of individual rights, and therefore our freedom.

The individual may act on his own volition, but a group must take direction.

The Takeaway for Freedom's Defense: The only entitlement in America is freedom.

Chapter 10

America *Is* Special

The Assault on Freedom: Multiculturalism undermines the truth of America by teaching the equality of cultures. All cultures have good and bad within them; but all cultures are not equally good nor equally bad.

America. Is she a special country? If America is special, what makes her so? Is it the people who founded her? Is that the source of her greatness, or is it something other? Could the same success America has enjoyed happen to any other group of people, or were these original American people special and somehow different than all the rest? In other words, is it the idea or founding of America that is somehow special and unique or is it something pertaining to her bloodline and therefore not necessarily available or possible for other people or cultures? A ruling bloodline kept the English and European kings, queens, dictators, and tyrants in power and a family affair for hundreds of years. This same hereditary notion of political power of the bloodline made and makes it certain that only the self-appointed elite would and will occupy the highest chairs of governmental power, and never the common man. In the old world of the pilgrims, one's birth for the most part, largely determined one's life and fate. Is this the case for America as well?

Governments have risen and fallen throughout the entire history of mankind. And with little exception blood has been spilled in the process. Revolution via blood-soaked soil is all too common in the history of man and man's government. The power of man ruling over man has been the goad, or motivation, of wars for thousands of years of human history. Many often seek to blame war on religion and or politics, but do they forget man animates religion and politics and not the other way around? Man seeking authority and control over man is the root cause of war, not religion and politics. These are the political covers or excuses given to gain popular public support which is needed to engage in war for power and control. Government power is a strong elixir and mankind has proven over and over he is willing to kill his fellowman or even his brother to achieve and keep it. On this basis, America, on the surface, certainly seems no different. She came to existence, in part, through the path of bloody revolution just like so many past governments.

> *Man seeking authority and control over man is the root cause of war, not religion and politics.*

The Just War theory, however, holds that men have a right to self defense of their natural God-given individual rights. Was the American Revolution, therefore, just? Or was the American Revolution no different than past bloody power grabs? Power grabs by one group or one man seeking power over another for power's sake? Thereby making America's government different but not necessarily any better than any other government structure? Or is it true that the American Revolution stands apart from all past revolutions? By extension of the Declaration of Independence, the American Constitutional government also stands apart and is somehow special. So is America really special and if this is true, then why?

In the following pages I will do my best to answer these questions of America and her founding. In order to do so it is necessary to turn the pages of history back to the time of the plight of the Protestant Reformation, Puritans, Pilgrims, American colonists, and those patriots who fought the American Revolution. For they, after all, are the reason America, and man's individual liberty, came to be.

The reformation or the individual right of conscious of man began in earnest when Martin Luther pounded by nail his famous 95 theses to the door of the Castle church in Wittenberg Germany on October 31, 1517. The 95 theses were 95 points that Luther held in criticism against the Catholic Church's teaching. Teaching that, according to Luther, the church used which abused and controlled the people. He used the Holy Scripture as his defense against the church in Rome. Imagine that, using the Bible as a defense of man's right of conscious against the church itself. The mind of man, or right of conscious, was held in bondage by the church and by the state. This was true of the institutions individually and as the church and state monolithically.

Several quotes help to establish the historical reality and context of our American forefathers and their struggle for freedom of conscience and independence.

The following words were written by William Bradford, Governor of Plymouth Plantation. He was speaking of the plight of the Pilgrims and their coming escape from tyranny in England to relative safety in Holland prior to their eventual departure to a land called America. Holland had a Republican form of government at the time. In other words, no king, queen, dictator, or tyrant. This was the period of 1607-1608. These words were written after the Pilgrims were discovered to be illegally meeting for church, against the orders of the King, at the Scrooby Manor House in Nottinghamshire England. The King allowed no right to assemble for the Pilgrims. Our founders would later, in our American constitution, legally recognized this individual right of assembly for all Americans.

> ...They (pilgrims) were hunted and persecuted on every side, until their former afflictions were but as fleabitings in comparison. Some were clapped into prison; others had their houses watched night and day, and escaped with difficulty; and most were obliged to fly, and

> leave their homes and means of livelihood...However, being thus molested, and seeing that there was no hope of their remaining there, they resolved by consent to go into the Low Countries, where they heard there was freedom of religion for all; and it was said that many from London and other parts of the country, who had been exiled and persecuted for the same cause, had gone to live at Amsterdam and elsewhere in the Netherlands.

Bradford continues,

> ...for though it was made intolerable for them to stay (in England), they were not allowed to go; the ports were shut against them, so that they had to seek secret means of conveyance, to bribe the captains of ships, and give extraordinary rates for their passages. Often they were betrayed, their goods intercepted, and thereby were put to great trouble and expense.[66]

The Protestant Christian Pilgrims were fleeing the almighty, tyrannical, and deadly union of the state established church and state itself. The Pilgrims simply wanted to live according to the dictates of their own consciences. Specifically, the Pilgrims sought to make interpretations of biblical scripture a matter of their own individual consciences. The Bible was not widely available for private reading in England until the 1560s and later. With the earlier invention of movable type by Johann Gutenberg, the Geneva Bible was first printed in Switzerland in 1560. The Geneva Bible, as it became known, was then smuggled to areas of Europe and England. For years anyone caught for simple possession of a Bible risked punishment by excommunication or possible burning at the stake. The church and state attempted full control of the dissemination and interpretation of religious writings. And between the two, the state ultimately controlled the church, although both wielded much authority which they comingled in order to maintain control and power over the people. For example, prior to the Geneva Bible, William Tyndale fervently desired to translate the Bible to English. He did so secretly in Cologne, Germany, in 1525. Tyndale Bibles were then illegally smuggled into England by various methods. For printing the Bible in English, William Tyndale was burned at the stake on October 6, 1536, for the charge of heresy. Heresy: daring to think for oneself and have an opinion different than the ruling authority. And, again, the ruling authority was the state and the state established church. Tyndale's last words were; "Lord, open the King of England's eyes."[67]

The Geneva Bible was a significant development because it was massed produced and made available to the general public. The Geneva Bible was thought of as a study Bible because it assisted the reader in cross-referencing various verses which contributed greatly to the individuals understanding of Bible scripture. No longer did the public have to rely on the Church and State to tell them what the scriptures said, or supposedly said as was the case at times.

In 1582 Queen Elizabeth made it illegal to worship in your own home and state church attendance was enforced by the Crown. The Black Acts were passed in 1584 which made King James the head of the Church in Scotland. This gave him total authority over all matters of the Church. In 1593, under Queen Elizabeth in England, the Act Against Puritans was passed by parliament. This act demanded full obedience to the Church of England or be forced to leave the realm, and forfeit all of your property to the Crown. Failure to do so was punishable by death.

The Kings and Queens used their power of the Crown and the state established Church to enforce political obedience to the Crown. Political obedience? Does that sound familiar? I hope you are beginning to see the nexus of the government coupled with the tactics, past and present, of those men and women who seek power over mankind. Political obedience to the Crown is today no different than Political Correctness. There is no difference and this movement against freedom must be stopped. You see how old these governmental tactics of political power are. When these tactics are being utilized and enforced by the political powers you know that liberty is being threatened. The tactics to enforce political obedience via political correctness are aimed directly at the heart of liberty. This direct historical link to political correctness should send chills down the spine of any American and liberty-loving person. I hope it does and I hope you are.

The tactics to enforce political obedience via political correctness are aimed directly at the heart of liberty.

What comes next is absolutely fascinating and shocking in light of what we are told currently of the separation of church and state. This is the critical point to grasp. Ready? The Protestant

Puritans, in the year 1604, beseeched King James for greater... "Separation of Church and State." This enraged King James as he believed he had a divine right to rule and be the head of the Church.

> "Thus the opponents, (Puritan Christians), of the (state established) Church became the sole guardians of popular liberty; the lines of the contending parties were distinctly drawn: the established church and the monarch, on the one side, were arrayed against the (protestant) Puritan clergy and the people."
>
> George Bancroft / Historian
> Founder U.S. Naval Academy in Annapolis, Maryland
> Vol. I ,1854 [68]

Commenting further on this period of King James and his oppressive rule, another historian, Reverend Mr. Cooper, writes the following in 1814, "...the government in church and state growing everyday more oppressive..." (*The History of North America*, Rev. Mr. Cooper / 1814.)[69]

That quote is from the 1814 edition of the historical account of North America by a Christian Reverend Mr. Cooper. By now it should be clear the original advocates of "separation of church and state" were the Protestant Christian Pilgrims. Protestant Christian Pilgrims first sought the removal of government shackles from the mind of man. The Christians coming out of the Protestant Reformation with the ability to read the scriptures for themselves for the first time, introduced the idea that all men are free and have no master but God. They believed 1) Man's rule over man is a false teaching, 2) man has no King but God, and 3) as some believe, a man who believes in no God has that right as well. This was the fight for the liberty of the mind of man. The right of conscience.

Unfortunately, because of the lack of teaching our true heritage and history, the progressive statist movement of big government over individual liberty and constitutional rights has successfully forged a false narrative that the Christian is the threat to separation of church and state. That the Christian, if allowed, will gain in political power and advance his beliefs through the force of the law. In the old world man used the Crown and man used the church to control man. History makes it clear. The man who desires to force his will or beliefs upon the rest of us in order to gain or otherwise maintain governmental power is the threat. It is not simply the vehicle that he chooses to use. Do not fear the vehicle necessarily; fear the man. However, the state is always used because the state is the source of legal power. The particular belief that gets coupled or linked to the power of the state depends upon the person(s) that seek to join their beliefs with the state. History shows that to join or co-mingle one's belief with the power of the state in order to impose one's will upon the people is the danger.

Any man who seeks to attach his personal beliefs to the power of the state to force his views upon other men is a threat to individual human liberty.

Unprincipled men of ill-repute, men of vice, or men of excessive zeal in their personal beliefs will use whatever vehicle necessary, including deception and force, to achieve their political aims. Any man who seeks to attach his personal beliefs to the power of the state to force his views upon other men is a threat to individual human liberty. It is not, therefore, church and state that is the threat to liberty—it is state established-belief and state that is the threat. The constant cry of the danger of the Christian church and state is a subtle and dishonest sleight of the historical hand. A deceptive perversion of the truth of history is used, in my opinion, to create the illusion that the Christian is the threat to liberty. This is a direct perversion of the historical record. It ought to serve as a clue to who may be the real threat. The Christian, atheist, agnostic, pagan, nor the secular humanist alone is not the threat per se. The threat is any man who seeks to enforce his belief upon the rest of us through the power of the law. That is the danger and threat to liberty. That is the lesson of the protestant reformation. This is why, I think, it is critical that a free people who intend to remain free must elect persons of high moral integrity who will not attempt to impose their will upon the rest of us through the power of the state. As a Christian I could have an atheist, although it would not be my choice, as President provided that he is a believer in man's constitutional individual liberty and does not use his belief combined with his power of state to force me to bend to his will. Likewise, if a Christian were elected by the people to be

President it is incumbent upon him to uphold the constitutional individual liberty for the atheist as well as anyone else that may differ in his right of conscience. This was the America of our Founders.

Because of their persecution the Puritans went into hiding and continued to meet in secret to hold church services at Scrooby Manor. In the year of 1604 approximately 300 Puritan pastors were jailed, silenced, or put in exile. King James put even more shackles upon them.

> The importation of foreign books was impeded; and a *severe censorship of the press* (italics added) was exercised by the bishops...Frivolous acts were denounced as ecclesiastical (Church) offenses. A later convocation, in a series of canons, denied every doctrine of popular rights, asserting the superiority of the King to the parliament and the laws, and admitting, in their zeal for absolute monarchy, no exception to the duty of passive obedience.
>
> George Bancroft / Historian
> Founder of U.S. Naval Academy in Annapolis Maryland
> Vol. I, 1854 [70]

Read that again, please. I hope you are beginning to see the why of the First Amendment and other amendments to our American constitution. The constitution is there to protect our individual rights from each other and ultimately from the government itself. The time for the Puritans to flee would soon be at hand.

> The Church of England...Being a *State established Church*, headed by the king or queen, controlled in its corporation by State mandates, the

> Church existed by permission of the civil government. If you lived or were born within a certain radius of a Church of England, you were automatically a member from birth to death and billed or tithed accordingly... the government controlled the Church, and the Church controlled the people…
>
> *Founders Bible*, page 97 [71]

The availability of the Bible cleared the way for believers to begin to read and study its writings for themselves. They no longer had to rely upon the Crown or church to tell them what the book said. Their growing biblical knowledge began to cast doubt on the divine right of Kings and therefore the power of the crown over man's conscience. They found this notion of divine rights to be false teaching and so they rightfully rebelled for their right to believe as they wished. To the Crown and its State Church of England, this was seen as a threat to its authority. This is why the Pilgrims were persecuted. The Crown and its State-controlled church in England feared, even though they could not possibly see the future, what eventually became the cause of the American Revolution. The freedom of mankind from under the control of man. This would mean the loss of the English Crown and its monarchial power as it has existed heretofore.

Thomas Paine would later put it this way. "The cause of America is in great measure the cause of all mankind."[72]

Pilgrims Flight from Tyranny to Liberty

It took two costly attempts, in monetary and human terms, for the Pilgrims to depart England for Holland. A third, if one is to count the final departure from Leiden, Holland, on the ship Speedwell, back to Southampton, England, for the Mayflower and finally off to America. I am writing here, however, of the first two attempts of the Pilgrims to flee England.

After the discovery of their illegal church meetings at the Scrooby Manor House it became obvious to the Pilgrims that fleeing the King's tyranny was their only option. An agreement was made with a sea captain from England and the plan was set. The Pilgrims sold their homes and other possessions in preparation for their escape. At the appointed time, the Pilgrims met their captain near Boston, England, and boarded the ship. The Pilgrims were promptly searched and arrested by the king's magistrates. They lost all the funds they acquired by selling their homes and other belongings. It seems that informing the King's authorities on Puritans was a good business and their sea captain double-crossed them and turned them in. They were put in prison. After about a month many were released but William Bradford and William Brewster were kept for a longer term. These events took place in late 1607.

The Pilgrims were not dismayed nor deterred from their desire for freedom. Later in 1608, after the release from prison of William Bradford and William Brewster, the Pilgrims planned another escape attempt. This time they hired a Dutch sea captain and once again the plan for escape was set. At the appointed hour the women and children were boarded into a small sailing vessel in a tidal creek leading to the open sea. They were to sail to open water and meet their Dutch captain and board the larger vessel at sea. The pilgrim men were traveling the distance to the sea on foot. The captain was late in arriving and the open sea being rough for the small sailboat carrying the women and children, they decided to come back in to calmer waters. This was a costly miscalculation. They were in tidal waters and became stranded by the ebb tide. Meanwhile, the Dutch captain finally arrived and most of the men boarded the ship. Then suddenly, Bradford writes, "the captain espied a large body of horse and foot, armed with bills and guns and other weapons, for the countryside had turned out to capture them." The captain having no choice "having fair wind, weighed anchor, hoist sail, and away!" continued Bradford. Now imagine the scene. The women and children, along with all of the pilgrim's money, were stuck on the hard in a shallow tidal zone. Some pilgrim men didn't make the boarding and were left on land painfully witnessing the events as they unfolded, while the other pilgrims were sailing off over the horizon to Holland. All of these events simultaneously occurring whilst the men, women, and children pilgrims were chased by the king's armed men.

A storm soon overtook the Dutch ship however, a bad storm. Hundreds of sailboats, it was later learned, were lost at sea. A half-day's sail across the English Channel took them 14 or more days because of the storm. Nevertheless, a partial success for the flight from tyranny was theirs. At long last, is was a real beginning of the road to liberty that changed the tide of history. The other men, women, and children pilgrims eventually made another successful attempt and all met, in due time, in Holland.

The struggle for the right of conscience has a long and bloody history. It is essentially the struggle for man to free himself from the will and control of man. It is the struggle for the individual freedom of humanity against those of the same species of humanity who perceive some high notion that they are to organize and control the rest of us in our beliefs and lifestyle. No man has any natural authority over another man and his beliefs. A full chapter is devoted to man's right of conscience. You will read of the tens of thousands of beheadings and burnings at the stake. All because some men and women will do anything to maintain power over others. This is not hyperbole. This is true history and descriptive of our current times as well. The reality of the dark side of man is that there are those who seek power and control over others. All men, nay most men, thank God, do not seek nor even ponder this type of power. But do not deceive yourself, some men and women do. There is nothing new under the sun.

The reality of the dark side of man is that there are those who seek power and control over others.

Years after the Pilgrims fled England the struggle of man's right of conscience and freedom continued to rage. Those kings, queens, dictators and tyrants, who have held power over man for centuries would not give it up for love and charity for mankind. Therefore, the struggle for man's freedom was a long and bloody path through the pages of history. One hundred and sixty-eight long years after the Pilgrims fled England the American Revolution began. Thomas Paine in *Common Sense* 1776, declared the following as the fight for man's freedom from man was still not finished. "O ye that love mankind! Ye that dare oppose, not only tyranny, but the tyrant, stand forth! Every spot of the old world is overrun with oppression. Freedom hath been hunted round the globe. Asia and Africa have long expelled her, Europe regards her like a stranger, and England hath given her warning to depart. O! receive the fugitive, and prepare in time an asylum for mankind."

"O ye that love mankind! Ye that dare oppose, not only tyranny, but the tyrant, stand forth! Every spot of the old world is overrun with oppression. Freedom hath been hunted round the globe. Asia and Africa have long expelled her, Europe regards her like a stranger, and England hath given her warning to depart. O! receive the fugitive, and prepare in time an asylum for mankind."
- Thomas Paine

America finally became mankind's asylum for freedom Paine so eloquently spoke of. The time before the Pilgrims and the time period between the plight of the Pilgrims and the American Revolution was long, difficult, and deadly. That difficult, deadly, and bloody battle for our freedom and right of conscience was fought against whom? Why, man himself. Why? Because some apparently believe it is their right, hereditary or otherwise, to rule over others. We, therefore, must understand our history so we can better comprehend and appreciate the depth of this gift of freedom; the fragility of this gift in light of those who would still deny it today; and our obligation to posterity to strengthen it once again; and to recognize how much of it has already been lost due to apathy, ignorance, lack of education, and also due to unconstitutional and illegal power grabs by some of those we have elected. This must be corrected before it is too late.

About 170 years passed between the Pilgrims' flight from tyranny in England until the American Declaration of Independence in 1776. This period was, in large part a continuation of government tyranny and abuse of power of the English kings, queens, and British colonial governors over the Colonies.

> England treated the settlers as an inferior class of people. Her intention was to make and keep the colonies dependent. The laws were framed to favor the English manufacturer and merchant at the expense of the colonist. The Navigation Acts compelled the American farmer to send his products across the ocean to England, and to buy his goods in British markets. American manufacturers were prohibited...Even William Pitt, the friend of America, declared

> America had no right to manufacture even a nail for a horseshoe, except by permission of Parliament.[73]

Barnes Historical Series continues to explains how King George III treated the colonists:

- **Writs of assistance** were passed by the crown whereby "any petty custom house official could enter a man's house or store at his pleasure."[74] The officials would do this in order to rifle through the belongings of the colonists. The British government allowed no right of privacy.
- **The Stamp Act** (1765) "ordered that stamps bought of the British government, should be put on all legal documents, newspapers, pamphlets, etc…"[75] This tax was expensive for the colonists.
- **The Mutiny Act** "ordered that the colonies should provide these British soldiers with quarters and necessary supplies… This evident attempt to enslave the Americans aroused burning indignation. To be taxed was bad enough, but to shelter and feed their oppressors was unendurable."[76]
- **The Boston Massacre**, March 5, 1770 the British soldiers fired on a crowd of colonists gathered to protest their presence. "A fight ensued, in which three colonists were killed and eight wounded."[77]

- **The Boston Tea Party**, December, 16, 1773 The British lifted some taxes but left the tax on tea. The colonists were tired of government rules, regulations, and games. "This subterfuge exasperated the patriots. They were fighting for a great principle..." The principle of individual liberty individual rights to live free from the tyranny of government of man. Thus, some patriots dressed as Indians and boarded a ship laden with tea in the Boston Harbor, and dumped all of the tea overboard. "A party of men, disguised as Indians, boarded the vessels and emptied three hundred and forty-two chests of tea into the water."[78]
- **Gun control ordered under King George III** - The patriots, led by George Washington, were victorious in the battle of Trenton on December 26, 1776. Upon victory during a search of the area it was found: "In a folio general-order book belonging to Col. Rhal's battalion, taken at Trenton... the following barbarous order is frequently repeated, "His Excellency the Commander-in-Chief orders, that all inhabitants (colonists) who shall be found with arms, not having an officer with them, shall be immediately taken and hung up." "These men are continually harping on the great sin of our bearing arms." Writes Thomas Paine in his book, *The American Crisis*.[79]

> *The master of government is the people—anything less and you have tyranny.*

The lines were now drawn and battles began even before the Declaration of Independence was declared on July 4, 1776. For example, there was the Battle of Lexington where the first American patriots were killed. There was the attack on Fort Moultrie in Charleston, SC, on June 28, 1776. *Barnes Historical Series* (1871) tell us: "So fearful was the response from Moultrie's guns, that, at one time, every man but Admiral Parker was swept from the deck of his vessel." The British "fleet was so shattered that it sailed for New York."[80] This was the South Carolina colonist's first encounter with the famed *Mistress of the Seas*, as the British Naval fleet was so dubbed. The SC colonists had a victory to claim. But, we are not talking of a victory over a bunch of man-o-war sail boats. We are talking about a victory over tyranny; man's freedom was at stake. South Carolina was energized by this victory. Everywhere were repeated the thrilling words of Patrick Henry, "Give me liberty or give me death." (Patrick Henry's speech in St. John's Church in Richmond Va.)

This gives you a sense of the great length of the hundreds of bloody years it took mankind to throw off the tyrant of man and fashion a just government by consent of the people. It has taken centuries from before the time of the pilgrims and until the American revolution for man to achieve a just government by consent of the governed which places the rights of the individual above the government. The master of government is the people—anything less and you have tyranny. It is then only a question of degree, a soft or hard tyranny. America is currently in a soft stage of tyranny. Government's sole purpose in these United States is to protect the individual rights of the people equally. Government's role is not to speak of us as separate groups and then divide us into class groups of rich and poor, the educated and the non-educated, upper class or lower class, this race and that, this minority or that. These divisions are then used by the unscrupulous politicians to agitate or compare one group to the next which causes discontent. Who is this tyrant of man? It is any man, woman, or group of men and women who seek to force their beliefs or will upon the rest of us through the power of the state. It is therefore, "state established belief and state." Any person's belief system coupled with the power of the state is the danger to individual liberty.

Please consider carefully what I am about to say. At any point throughout the history of mankind any one of the kings, queens, dictators or tyrants could have quit the throne, so to speak, and declared all men to be created equal. Any one of them could have declared all men equal to the king or queen and all men have the same God-given rights. This did not happen—ever. Why? Because power over others is a very commanding position and difficult to resist for most men. Especially power of government over others. Who would give up the power to legally force people to bend to your will? What kind of person could resist this powerful temptation? Especially to give it up for the purpose of sharing that power among the people equally. And then to enshrine this act of love of fellowman with the words, "We hold these truths to be self evident: that all men are created equal: that they are endowed by their Creator with certain unalienable rights." I'll tell you who, Men of a highly-cultivated sensitivity to moral integrity that nurtured within themselves a love of their neighbor as they love themselves. The freedom of man from government, since the fall of Adam through the plight of the Pilgrims, never saw the light of day until the American Revolution and the Founding Fathers created the American Constitution. This was the first and only constitution to place man in charge of his own individual person and above his government.

The freedom of man from government, since the fall of Adam through the plight of the Pilgrims, never saw the light of day until the American Revolution and the Founding Fathers created the American Constitution.

Patrick Henry is credited with saying, "The Constitution is not an instrument for the government to restrain the people, it is an instrument for the people to restrain the government - lest it come to dominate our lives and interests."

Consent of the governed means that government is the servant of man and not the other way around. In America after a long and painful struggle, the freedom of man was finally held high and brought forth from the bloody gauntlet of history to America. This is no trifle matter. This is a grave and reverent matter in regard to humanity and its rightful God-given freedom. America, for the first time in history threw the King of England off the throne in America and, therefore, off the back of man. Kings, queens, dictators, and tyrants in America were replaced with nature's law and nature's God as the only master of man.

In *Common Sense 1776,* Thomas Paine said, "But where, some say, is the King in America? I'll tell you, friend, he reigns above, and doth not make a havoc of mankind like the Royal brute of Britain...let a crown be placed thereon, by which the world may know, that so far as we approve of monarchy, that in America THE LAW IS KING."

Then, in America, through the love of fellowman, man gave the greatest gift to man from man in the history of humanity. That gift was the gift of individual human liberty with the legal and constitutional recognition of individual equal rights for all. When man unseated the tyrant king this was a victory of man over man. But the victory in America was that victory and one giant victorious step more. In America man overcame himself when he granted equality of rights and liberty to all. Our Founding Fathers did what no king, queen, dictator, tyrant, progressive, statist, or state established church would ever do. After a long bloody and victorious revolution for the cause of freedom for mankind they stepped back from the seat of power and handed the power of government to the people. This was a monumental moment in the history of mankind. Man triumphed over himself through love of his fellowman. This recognition of self evident truths enabled our founders not to seek the throne themselves but to legally enshrine and share this victory for all men through our American constitution. Equal individual rights for all. It was a common bow of love of man toward man in full recognition that man has no King but God. And that my dear friend, is why...America is Special.

Daniel Webster said, “Hold on my friends, to the constitution and to the Republic for which it stands. Miracles do not cluster, and what has happened once in 6,000 years, may not happen again. Hold on to the Constitution, for if the American Constitution should fail, there will be anarchy throughout the world.”[81]

A Farewell Warning From Our First President

Our first President, George Washington, in his September 17, 1796 Farewell Address, gave many warnings to the people about unscrupulous men or politicians who would use whatever means necessary to usurp the constitution and our individual rights in order to regain government control over man once again. He spoke of factions or groups that would cause division. Washington writes of them: “They are likely, in the course of time and things, to become potent engines, by which cunning, ambitious, and unprincipled men will be able to subvert the power of the people, and to usurp for themselves the reins of government; destroying afterward the very engines which have lifted them to unjust dominion." Once unscrupulous men gain power over a free state by manipulation of that state's free and open access to power, they then burn the ladder behind them. As Washington said "destroying afterwards the very engines which have lifted them to unjust dominion."[82]

The Good Cause Method of Usurpation

Continuing, Washington, says that "One method of assault may be to effect in the forms of the Constitution, alterations which will impair the energy of the system, and thus to undermine what cannot be directly overthrown."[83] He further warned of manipulation of the constitution "that you resist with care the spirit of innovation upon its principles, however specious the pretexts."[84] So no matter how good the cause sounds, unscrupulous men will use these good-sounding causes to usurp or alter our founding principles. People will use causes that most all of us would deem good, kind, loving, caring, etc. to expand government power and thereby diminish individual liberty. For example, the "poor" is for how many years been cited as a worthy cause for government assistance. And the poor are still with us. The cause needs attention for sure, but it is not the function of the federal government to give it. Causes like the poor are causes that a moral and just citizenry

The welfare state has only proved to place certain individuals and groups in a perpetual state of welfare.

must take upon themselves to offer aid, education, and assistance. Many private organizations are already doing this. Imagine if private organizations had the money that government has wasted on "good causes." Government, for many reasons, is not the vehicle for such causes. Just because I believe a cause is a good cause, that does not give me the right to take your money and spend it the way I wish. What one person may consider a good cause another may not. The welfare state has only proved to place certain individuals and groups in a perpetual state of welfare. Then they become dependent upon their supporting counterparts in government who gain perpetual election, it seems, by this unholy alliance of mutual dependency. This is actually cruel and places these people as expenditures of the politically greedy class. It is a crafty political triangulation maneuver between the politically greedy class, the poor (who are used in the worst way by the politically greedy class), and the law abiding hard working producers who are forced to fund the whole enterprise. The producers are also being used by the politically greedy class. These poor are, in other words, used not helped. Thomas Jefferson, our third president, is said to have put it this way:

> "The democracy will cease to exist when you take away from those who are willing to work and give to those who would not." "My reading of history convinces me that most bad government results from too much government."

Washington is warning us that this will happen and when it does we must resist changing our founding principles. We must recognize deceptive, subversive attempts at "fundamental transformation" for what they are—attempts to undermine our founding principles of freedom. America is a country founded on principles of individual freedom. When you create groups and undermine these principles of individual liberty, you are undermining your own freedom. Principles are axiomatic, universal, and eternal. Principles being eternal truths and unchanging, therefore offer us a stable platform for our government. Whims of whatever fancy, pop culture philosophy, or the popular good cause of the day are always in flux and are not therefore stable platforms for government to be built upon. They are the rungs in the ladder to despotic power that George Washington warns us of. Washington further writes and speaks of *factions*, or divisions; "It agitates the community with ill-founded jealousies and false alarms - kindles the animosity of one party against another, foments occasionally riot and insurrection. It opens the door to foreign influence and corruption, which find a facilitated access to the government itself through the channels of party passion. Thus the policy and the will of one country are subjected to the policy and will of another."[85]

Washington goes on to warn that this is the road to ruin of our republic. "The disorders and miseries which result, gradually incline the minds of men to seek security and repose in the absolute power of an individual; and sooner or later the chief of some prevailing faction...turns this disposition to the purposes of his own elevation, on the ruins of public liberty."[86] Now I ask you, are we not living the precise days of peril that our beloved first President warned us of? For myself, I find this truth to be self-evident and astounding in its prophetic accuracy.

The good cause method of usurpation has many masks, one of which, aid to the poor, was spoken of earlier. Here are a few others: national security, your health, your safety, the economy, the environment, education, world hunger, etc. These are important issues but that is not the point. Washington was warning us about that "cunning, ambitious, and unprincipled men, will be able to subvert the power of the people, and to usurp for themselves the reins of government." The use of "good causes," that are worthy of human energy and attention, is how government too often manipulates our emotions to increase its power. The problem is the government takes up good causes that are not within

When the private sector voluntarily gives aid to needy causes, as it should in a moral society, there is no corresponding growth of government and no individual freedom is lost.

its constitutional powers, usurping authority not granted them. The result is a net gain of increased power for the government and a net loss of individual freedom for the people. When a principled man steps forward and speaks against a government program for the poor, that man is singled out, ridiculed, and castigated for being calloused, cold hearted, and uncaring for the poor. He was not speaking out against helping the poor, but only the practice of handing that job to the government. The unscrupulous ones George Washington spoke of will use these causes and deceptive tactics to grow the power of the federal government.

When the private sector voluntarily gives aid to needy causes, as it should in a moral society, there is no corresponding growth of government and no individual freedom is lost. By contrast when the people hand these duties over to the government, the government unconstitutionally by fiat expands its power to appear to solve the problem. The result—government power is expanded, individual freedom lost through regulation and taxation, and the problem is generally never resolved. Think about this; if the government actually solved the particular problem, what would be the result? The politicians would put themselves out of business. The politicians want to perpetuate problems while only appearing to solve them because it is in their best interests. Not to mention the unconstitutionality of the government taking on good causes. This kind of chicanery would never survive in the private sector economy and the people and problems would get the real attention and help that they need.

Thus the thrust of our first President, George Washington's, farewell warning is this:

1. Be on guard for cunning, unprincipled, crafty, politicians, that will divide the people against themselves. These crafty men (community organizers) will divide and prod the people until "It agitates the community with ill-founded jealousies and false alarms - kindles the animosity of one party against another, foments occasionally riot and insurrection."[87]
2. These unscrupulous men or women will seek to undermine the constitution (much in this regard has already occurred). Washington warned us of "One method of assault may be to effect in the forms of the constitution, alterations which will impair the energy of the system, and thus to undermine what cannot be directly overthrown." We are overrun with government regulation and bureaucracy which has damaged our capitalistic economy. Or in Washington's words again: "alterations which will impair the energy of the system... to undermine what cannot be directly overthrown."[88] This was Washington's warning that crafty, ill-intended, men will over time seek the fundamental transformation of America.

3. Washington went on to state that the outcome of these assaults on our liberty will be the cause of "The disorders and miseries which result" and finally the fatigues of economic and other miseries will "...incline the minds of men to seek security and repose in the absolute power of an individual; and sooner or later the chief of some prevailing faction... turns this disposition to the purposes of his own elevation..."[89] In other words, Washington warned of the path of man controlling man in America through a gradual process of creating misery which leads people to cry out for a strong individual to just "fix it," which results in the "absolute power of an individual."
4. This, he warns will result in "...the ruins of public liberty."[90] I think we are living the days of Washington's warning. What do you think?

Man Wants His Throne Back

Man has ruled man for most all of human history. The only exception is America as founded. Our Constitution which created this land of freedom is a mere 240 years old. The human history of man ruling man is thousands of years old by comparison. America dethroned the rule of man over man for the first time in all of human history. This is why America is called the 6,000-year miracle. The next time you hear the sophomoric argument that America's constitution is old and therefore must be replaced, remember and respond with what you just read. The wheel is much older than our constitution and still in use. Should we abandon it, based upon its age? This line of reasoning is illogical and absurd. Ideas are replaced by better ideas and age has nothing to do with it. In this regard, I know of no better idea than our constitution which is based upon God-given individual human freedom; do you?

You should be aware that there is a 120-plus-year-old movement in America, progressivism, to eradicate any and all vestiges of nature and nature's God from our government, schools, public squares, etc. This would subvert and destroy our entire constitutional system if it were to succeed. This movement has already claimed many victories. Nature hates a vacuum and the successful subversion of our country's founding principles, grounded in nature and nature's God, will leave a vacuum that will be filled with non-principled arbitrary and unstable pop-culture-politics. Man would then be on the throne in America replacing nature and nature's God. This would be tantamount to the reversal of the American Revolution. Those that seek to deny God and eternal natural law undermine mankind's powerful and profound argument for human freedom. That argument for individual human freedom is rooted upon the self-evident laws of nature and nature's God. Human freedom and the concept of nature and nature's God are inexorably linked. Each man individually has certain unalienable natural and or God-given rights. I do not get my rights from you and you don't get your rights from me. Therefore, I cannot take your rights from you and you cannot take my rights from me. All men being equal, which man among us is worthy to step forward to claim his authority to tell the rest of us what our rights are? No man has this authority. Your rights are a natural part of your human existence just as mine and your neighbors are. If one says, "I don't believe in God," that is his right of conscience and choice, but he still has the same protection of his natural rights as all the rest. No more and no less.

America was founded upon Christian principles. America's founders were mostly Christian although they certainly had differing views of their beliefs just as people do today. This is the state of man.

> "In this age there can be no substitute for Christianity...That was the religion of the Founders of the republic and they expected it to remain the religion of their descendants."
>
> (United States Congress, 1854 / 33rd U.S. Congress)[91]

John Jay, 1st Justice of the U.S. Supreme Court and author of the *Federalist Papers*, writes, "Unto Him who is the author and giver of all good, I render sincere and humble thanks for His manifold and unmerited blessings, and especially for our redemption and salvation by His beloved son...Blessed be His holy name."[92]

George Washington, first President of the United States said, "Of all the dispositions and habits which lead to political prosperity, (Christian) religion and morality are indispensable supports. In vain would that man claim the tribute of patriotism, who should labor to subvert these great pillars."[93]

Nevertheless, have you ever noticed that the term in our founding documents, nature and nature's God was never defined as to which God are we talking about. In the case of the Pilgrims forward to the founders it is obvious that Christianity was the dominant spiritual view. Christian morality and biblical laws supporting man's freedom are a key bulwark to our founding principles. This is a matter of historical fact. I believe it directly contributed to our country's success. Nevertheless, it was not intended to be defined by the government because that fill-in-the-blank is reserved to each individual and his right of conscience. Because we are a nation founded upon Christian principles does not mean the one must be a Christian and cannot be an atheist with the same individual rights as all the rest. In fact, it guarantees just that. Under the umbrella of protection of nature and nature's God all men are protected in their belief system. All men from Christian, to atheist, agnostic, pagan, and one's lifestyle that springs from these fundamental and foundational personal choices. For example, gay, straight, whatever way you choose to pursue your happiness is strictly up to you and your conscience beliefs. All men are free under the notion of nature and nature's God to make these personal choices for themselves. Natural law and nature's God is the foundation for our right of conscience. It is what the Pilgrims to the Patriots fought for. It is the foundation of separation of *state established belief and state*. It is the root or basis of our individual freedom. Natural law is, therefore, the barrier to the man who would gain the power of the state and then fuse his belief with that state power in an effort to control the rest of us. Natural law is the very basis that forbids the government from trampling your natural right to free speech, for example. The Constitution states our individual liberties but our liberties are based upon natural law and nature's God. Natural God-given liberties that the government must not be allowed to alter.

The answer to nature and nature's God is an individual personal point to ponder, weigh, consider, and conclude for oneself. This demonstrates the magnitude, gravity, and freedom granting importance of those great words *nature and nature's God*. The government structure does not mean that anyone is or should be compelled to believe in God, much less which god. This structure of government based upon natural law is the basis for the principle of the rightful freedom of man to keep man or woman off the throne in America forever. Christianity, for example, may be privately suggested or highly recommended by some but that is a private matter and of no purview of the state. Washington and other founders did warn however that our system of freedom depends greatly upon the morality of our people. That is, in great measure, what is meant by and needed for self-government. Morality plays a key role toward the keeping of peace in our country and Christian religion plays a key role in morality.

Have you noticed the recent and sometimes fierce debate over church and state? If you recall from earlier in this chapter, the Protestant Christians or Pilgrims first fought this battle against the state and the state established church. But ironically today the Christian Church is often castigated for supposedly intruding into the sanctuary of separation of church and state. This is absurd in the light of history. It is a ruse, an attempt at deception of the highest order, by crafty souls for the goal of removing as much of Christianity or God from the American culture as possible thereby putting man back on the throne to rule man. I believe I have adequately supported the claim that without the man of high moral integrity there would be no America. You may recall that no king, queen, dictator, socialist, communist, or tyrant, state established belief or church ever abdicated his power, put it in a written constitution, and granted it to all the people *equally*. So, once again, the notion that the church is the threat to belief and state is historically false and a diversion. I have supported the case that it is man and his belief that is the threat to human liberty, if coupled to the power of the state. The inaccurate attack on the Christian Church in the matter of separation of church and state is a red herring or decoy to divert from the real threat. The phrase church and state is, in many ways, a misnomer in itself and misleading. As has been previously discussed the threat to freedom is belief and state no matter the source of the belief. The real threat is secular humanism and materialism through the progressive statist or socialist movement and I will explain why. To illustrate the point and show the real current threat to separation of belief and state, I offer the following quotes from the *Humanist Manifesto*.

> "Humanism asserts that the nature of the universe depicted by modern science makes unacceptable any supernatural or cosmic guarantees of human values."
>
> "...humanists still believe that traditional theism, especially faith in the prayer-hearing God, assumed to love and care for persons, to hear and understand their prayers, and to be able to do something about them, is an unproved and outmoded faith..."
>
> "No deity will save us; we must save ourselves."
>
> "If we are to solve our global problems, nation-states must transfer some of their sovereignty to a system of transnational authority."[94]

The secular humanist believes there is no natural law, there are no self-evident truths of nature and nature's God. To the humanist, morality is relative not absolute or universal. This humanist notion undermines the very fundamental principles undergirding our individual rights which keep man off the throne. The humanist believes that man through government alone will solve the problems of man. The humanist declares in his own words through the manifesto that it is humanist belief and state that is the salvation of man. In their own manifesto and in their own words, "No deity will save us; we must save ourselves." It is the secular humanist and materialist that is the threat to man's liberty and right of conscience via their disregard for any separation of belief and state. What they propose in their manifesto is a totalitarian global government. In other words, a return of man, humanist man, to the throne. Their weapons of choice to assault natural law and implement political correctness and social justice.

I, as a Constitution-believing American, make no argument against the humanists' right to believe as he wishes. The prior quotes are not for that purpose at all. The quotes support the claim that those men who wish to tell the rest of us what we can and cannot do exist. What we can and cannot believe. The quote is to stand as proof and warning that the wolves against man's freedom are ever at the gate, just as George Washington warned.

We are witnessing man's attempt to dethrone nature and nature's God in order to once again regain the throne for man in its stead. If there are no laws of nature and nature's God, then there can be no inalienable rights. If there are no inalienable rights then man can once again tell man what to do. If this fallacious ruse is allowed to prevail and the notion of nature and nature's God is somehow subverted, then man will have succeeded in recapturing the throne and the cause of America and man's freedom will have ended. It will truly be a case of back to the future and man will once again be ruled by man. We must not fail to recognize this threat is real. Moreover, we must recognize the truth and profound wisdom in our Constitution in that it actually protects man from man and man from the government of man.

> *History does not repeat itself—man repeats history*

The more knowledge one has of history the more one is able to fully comprehend and appreciate this momentous and magnanimous act of humanity towards humanity that occurred in America. Knowledge of history breathes life into the present. In the literal and figurative sense, power was ripped from the King's throne and handed to the people in a just war. I have no words to fully describe this moment in the history of mankind. We bear a serious and profound responsibility to uphold the freedom of man for those who are to come after us.

It is often said history repeats itself. I have a different take: history does not repeat itself—man repeats history. I believe this to be the case because the beneficiaries of success, us, are often not the same group of brave souls that strove, bled, and died to make that success possible. Over time passions fade, memories fail, and spring flowers return to the soil giving way to the summer heat and time moves on. Flowers, unlike man, are coded by nature and nature's God to return each spring to their glory and beauty. But man returns each epoch of history to stumble over the same log in the trail of life as if he had never seen it before. He does this without purposeful study of those before us, especially of such a great cause as we are discussing, without love for each other as ourselves, without principle. Man is not stupid, man is brilliant, but man often seeks the path of least resistance. This is because the decisions that man makes are a direct product of the values man cultivates. And herein lies the danger to posterity regarding the freedom of mankind. The danger is that we the beneficiaries of man's natural right to freedom fail to recognize, live, and teach, the eternal principles of freedom and we lose it for posterity due to apathy and ignorance. We are the beneficiaries of perhaps the greatest gift and cause ever accomplished by man—the cause of freedom of man from man. We therefore have a great and serious responsibility to our children and future generations to pass on the constitutional freedom we have been gifted.

The Takeaway for Freedom's Defense: America *is* special because America rescued the self-evident sovereign rights of man *from* government.

Chapter 11

Faith Is the Logical Choice

The Assault on Freedom: The assault on nature's God and natural law in America undermines our founding—that we are endowed by our Creator with certain self-evident inalienable individual rights.

There exists, in some circles of thought, a bifurcation, division, separation, or diametrical opposition between God on the one hand, and science on the other. This school of thought also includes the idea that science is for the logical man of reason, and God or faith is for the faithful who are willing to accept or believe in God without the reasoned and empirical evidence to back it up. In short, this school of thought advances that science is rational and faith is not. It follows from there that men of faith are somehow less rational compared to those who do not believe. The faithful have always seemed to acquiesce to this position as if it were true. The reasoned evidence available to man shows this entire claim to be false.

I have not pondered this argument over the years because I am not sure how to make rational or logical sense of the matter. I have pondered this notion because I cannot comprehend the basis for the question of this view in the first place. I considered the issue, not for the purpose of refuting it but for the reason of attempting to support the claim intellectually. I could not. I have, in other words, never held this view nor have I ever struggled with the notion of God and science being somehow at odds. Perhaps I am the 40-watt bulb in a room with 100-watters, but I just do not get it. Maybe a 40-watt bulb cannot see what a 100-watt bulb can see. Each of us has what we have by "gift" of nature and nature's God, so there is nothing for any man to be ashamed of whether he was given a little or a lot in intellectual ability or some other talent. Likewise, there is nothing for the brighter bulbs to boast over either because all of life is a gift.

Truth is its own defense—only the lie needs assistance.

I have lived long enough to know that all men do not seek truth. Some men try only to win, control, or dominate an argument. Truth is its own defense—only the lie needs assistance. Truth is a pathway, and that pathway leads somewhere. Some, perhaps, do not like where it leads. I don't know. Nevertheless, the intellectual pursuit of truth matters in the world of man because truth matters to all mankind. Truth is a stable platform from which man can build around and upon. Anything less is unstable, and therefore ultimately harmful. This is true whether we are talking about truth in science, government, jurisprudence, or faith. The challenge is to not block the pathway with your passion, biases, or preconceived notions. That is relatively easy when you don't have any particular interest in the subject matter. The challenge lies in keeping the light of truth on the pathway when the subject matter is dear to you.

I have always privately tried to use this method as a check upon myself and my ability to seek truth and not let myself get in the way of truth's path. In my experience, the criminal, wrongdoer, agenda, or philosophical worldview-driven man, does not like too many questions by honest men seeking truth, while the upright man welcomes or even prefers it. A truth-seeking man does not need to fear being wrong because he knows correcting it is an opportunity to be right.

If there is science, with all its laws, that can somehow stand alone absent a causal agent in this universe then there can be no God.

But back to the question of God vs. science, this is how I see the matter. First, if one accepts the argument as constructed, the bifurcated view that the two are separate entities, God loses at the outset. The moment you agree to a division between the two entities God cannot exist. If there is science, with all its laws, that can somehow stand alone absent a causal agent in this universe then there can be no God. For what kind of God would there be that did not create everything including science? If God did not create science, then God is not in control or the author of science. This would mean that there are things existing, independent of God, that God did not create. If there are things God did not create, how then can there be God? Would God, if God exists, not be the creator and sustainer of everything?

Therefore, at this point, I think it can be concluded there is no possibility of a bifurcated or separate existence between God and science. There is God and science together or just science existing alone without God. The notion of the two existing independently of one another is, in other words, a fallacy.

Of the notion of there just being science alone and no God. This view is essentially the view of Darwinian evolution or materialism. Materialism is the concept that nothing exists beyond the material world. An emotion, according to materialism, like love, joy, or hate, is not spiritual but a mere chemical reaction and nothing more. In this sense of evolution, I am speaking of the view of evolution which holds there is no God or belief in God. To me, one does not negate the other, but some argue the contrary. I do not disbelieve that evolution simply means change, to evolve. A male child, for example, evolves, changes or grows into an old man, provided life allows. Or the metamorphosis of the caterpillar into the monarch butterfly, or one breed of dog from another, to offer a couple of other examples. This, to me, in no way negates the notion of there being God. If, however, by evolution one means some self or spontaneous creation of life from a state of nothing to something and then from the inanimate to the animate, or an ordering of matter absent a supreme conscious being, I am of a different school of thought.

For the moment, rather than pursuing the question of the existence of God as creator of the universe directly, let's explore the question from an indirect angle. Let's look at it from the angle of man and nature as creators. To illustrate the point, consider the following. Let's say there are three general orders or categories to the universe and all are ultimately subject to the third order.

First, there is the natural order of things as man finds them in nature. The moon in the heavens above. The sand on the beach or desert for example. The sand of a desert or beach has its natural order affected only by the weather and waves which are also part of the natural order.

Second, there is the Human order or human creation, if you will allow. These are the things man creates out of the matter available to him and the laws that govern this matter, which is also discoverable and available for man's use.

Third, there is the Divine Order. This would include the universe and all things in it including man. It also includes, albeit indirectly, all the things man makes, discovers, or invents. The third order is the highest order and is supreme, and ultimately, in control over the first two. Evidence and reason, I think, support this claim and show it to be the case. You can decide for yourself whether or not you think that is true, and if I have succeeded or failed in that effort. So let's get started.

There are three levels of order. The natural order, the human order, and the Divine order. In other words, there is the natural order or design of things, the human order or design of things, and the Divine order or design of things.

First, I will give an example of natural order or design, then move to an example of human order or design. We can then compare and contrast these two orders of our natural and human world. The idea is to compare and contrast what nature makes or manufactures, if you will, to what man makes or manufactures and note the differences or similarities. For this example, I have selected glass. Glass makes a suitable object for this example because it is found in the natural order of things, as well as in the human order of things. Glass forms, or is made, naturally in nature. Nature's glass is called obsidian. Obsidian is formed when silica (sand) is spewed forth in a volcanic blast. Obsidian comes in a variety of colors but the most common color is black, and some of it is translucent. Obsidian is found at or near the edge of lava flows. Nature's design of obsidian is irregular shapes and blobs of volcanic glass. The shapes are called natural shapes since they are made by nature absent any consciousness. The shapes and sizes of the deposits are what one would expect from a mindless volcanic blast, random and highly irregular.

Now let's move to the human order or design of things. Again with glass, for consistency of our example. Early man used obsidian to make cutting tools such as spear points, arrowheads, and knives. Modern man uses obsidian to make medical scalpels. Medical scalpels made of obsidian are proven, in controlled trials, to be sharper cutting and capable of creating finer edges than medical quality steel. Nevertheless, to keep the analogy consistent, I will use the kind of glass that man makes and the things that man makes from that glass. Man-made glass is also made of sand similar to obsidian. Man has learned how to make glass in many color varieties as well. As we have seen, nature blasts out its volcanic glass in a variety of random shapes and sizes. Nature does not produce regular shapes in its glass, nor make the same shape twice. Man-made glass, unlike nature's glass, is mostly made of contemplated and purposeful regular shapes. It is also mostly produced with the modern molding tools to make the same precise shape over and over. As an example, let's go with your favorite beverage bottle. Man makes this bottle over and over again by the millions. Man produces the replicated beverage bottle one exact copy after another, day in and day out.

Therefore, the two types or categories of shapes, are the consistently irregular and random shapes which nature produces, and the man-made shapes which tend to be consistent and exact copies reproduced one after the other, as in our beverage bottle example. Two questions I think, at this time, need to be asked.

They are 1. Can man make what nature makes out of glass, and why or why not? 2. Can nature make what man makes out of glass, and why or why not?

So, can man make what nature makes out of glass? Specifically, can man create a machine that would spew and or thrust out molten glass to make blobs of random non-replicated objects of glass, just like nature? I think the answer is self-evident. The answer is yes. Man can make or create a very similar result to nature's volcanic glass.

So, can nature make what man makes out of glass? Specifically, can nature design, create, produce regular and precise shapes of glass like our beverage bottle and then replicate and reproduce the beverage bottle over and over and over by the millions. Again, I think the answer is self-evident. The answer is no. Nature cannot make beverage bottles nor can nature replicate the common beverage bottle. Nature cannot make one beverage bottle much less a single or million copies of that beverage bottle. Nature cannot reproduce what it cannot make in the first place.

We now have a clear distinction between the natural order or design, and the human order or design. This distinction is nature's irregular blob of glass and man's bottle. The distinction serves as a clarifying agent or light upon the path to help us find our way. At this point, another question comes to mind and begs asking. That question, it seems to me, is Why? Why the difference? Why can't nature do what man can do? Why? After all, the ingredients of glass come from nature. Why then can't nature make a beverage bottle and replicate it as man can? Nature is physically stronger than man for sure, so it is not a matter of physical ability or strength. What can man do that nature can't to make the beverage bottle?

Fundamentally, what is the difference between man and nature? Man comes from nature and is made up of component elements found in nature. But the elements of man or the bottle alone can't be the answer needed to solve the riddle. So why? What is it about man that allows him, the physically weaker between the two, to make the beverage bottle when nature cannot?

The difference is that man has conscious. Man has a mind, is self-aware, and can think. Man can contemplate concepts, has ideas of sundry variety, and can learn. Man can create the bottle because man can conceive the purpose and concept of the bottle and conceive of the machinery to make or create the bottle. Man, when he is alive, is animate. Nature's matter is inanimate, always. Man is animate, has cognition and creative abilities, and nature does not. Man thinks, and nature does not. Now we have arrived at another clear distinction between the natural order or design and the human order or design. Man's capacity to think or reason is the distinguishing characteristic between man and nature. Consciousness is the agent of life that allows man to produce or make what nature or the lower animals cannot. Moreover, it should not escape one's notice that while man can make the bottle, he cannot make the sand from which the bottle comes. Nature's God provides the sand and the science, and man provides the idea and creation of the bottle. Moreover, since matter nor its governing laws of science can be neither created or destroyed by man or nature, we can then conclude that neither were made by man nor nature. What exists, exists. No more and no less as far as man has control.

For a humorous view to make a serious point, imagine that nature could do what man can. Imagine that volcano spewing out your favorite beverage bottle one after another, or perhaps various glass decorations, or automobile windshields. This is a funny thought, but it serves a real purpose to the argument. If nature did this what would be the source of its ability to conceive of the objects it is producing? It would change your view of nature, would it not? Nature would be thinking or conscious, would it not? But, nature cannot do this because nature is not alive in the sense that man is alive. Nature obeys the laws of the universe that govern it because it must, but it is not aware of it doing so. Gravity returns the thrown rock to earth, but neither gravity nor the rock is aware of either's obedience to the laws of nature. Moreover, nature cannot utilize the natural laws of science in the ways that man can. Man has some range of liberty in his

Gravity returns the thrown rock to earth, but neither gravity nor the rock is aware of either's obedience to the laws of nature.

ability to creatively utilize the natural laws. Thus, we call the items made by man "man-made." The bottle is a man-made conscious creation, while the random blob of obsidian is naturally made. One is made by conscious creative utilization of the laws of nature, the bottle. While the other, obsidian rock, is made by nature without thought or consciousness but rather strict obedience to the laws of nature which nature itself is bound to obey.

It is certainly true that from dust to dust comes and goes man. All of the physical matter that makes up the human body is, after all, also found in our natural world. The human body is made up of certain elements and trace elements. The primary elements in the human body are oxygen, carbon, hydrogen, nitrogen, calcium, phosphorus, potassium, sulfur, sodium, chlorine, magnesium, and various other traces of elements. Even though the physical ingredients of man are known and are available in nature thus to nature and also to man, neither nature or man can produce an animated organic living breathing being. That animating, consciousness giving element of man is not listed among the natural elements of man. So what is it? How did it get there? Where did it come from? The prior parts of this discussion have shown that consciousness, along with matter and the associated laws of nature or science, are prerequisite or required to create a contemplated order or purposeful design from the natural order or nature. In others words our "bottle." It takes consciousness to create the bottle. That is why nature and matter, on its own, cannot

Nature can make a glass blob but not a bottle, man can make a glass blob and a bottle, but neither nature nor man can make a man.

create a bottle. The bottle is therefore unnatural. So here we are. Nature can make a glass blob but not a bottle, man can make a glass blob and a bottle, but neither nature nor man can make a man.

So what of man himself? What is the difference between man and the third level of order or design? Man has discovered the physical elements of his natural body, so why can't man make man from the knowledge of these elements? Why can't man make any animated organic living breathing being for that matter? What about a squirrel or a simple earthworm?

We now we have a third distinction between the natural order, the human order, and the divine order. The natural and human orders can make some things as we have already discussed. Namely the glass bottle and the glass blob. Nature has no mind or conscious while the human and Divine do. But there is a difference there too. That difference is that neither the natural order nor the human order can make organic animated living breathing beings. Not to mention, a living breathing being that has consciousness. Nature cannot do it and neither can man. An odd limitation, especially since nature has the elements and man knows what these elements are. Even with that knowledge, neither can put those elements together in a designed, purposeful molecular order that will produce an organic living breathing being. Man's reason, does it not, here evidences that man is not omniscient nor omnipotent over all aspects of man's known world.

Man and nature, it seems, are limited to making only non-organic inanimate non-breathing things. Yes, there are man-made robots, computers, and numerous and marvelous inventions of man, etc. but there are no organic beings made by mankind. Thus nature and man's ability to make or create certainly appear to each have their individually defined limits. If one is thinking of procreation of man or beast that is a different matter. Procreation is the act of continuing something previously created. Procreation is not an act of original creation in and of itself. We are talking about the first man, the first squirrel, the first earthworm, etc. And then, adding the ability to procreate. Nature has all the needed elements to evolve a man or squirrel, but it does not do so. Why? As was stated earlier, even though man knows the elements of his physical composition, man cannot make a man. Even less, man cannot create organic living breathing life and then give it consciousness—the ability to think.

The same for the bottle of man, but nature does not produce bottles either. Man can make a bottle, but man can't make a man even when the elements are known and available. I am arguing that there is another agent of creation not available to man or nature. What is it? What is that spark of life, the animating agent that distinguishes man and beast from the mound of dirt or the blob of glass? That essence that breathes the spirit of life into man. It is similar, I would think, to the agent of consciousness that allows and enables man to make the bottle when neither nature nor the lower animals can. It is similar but not the same. Man is but a mere image or shadow of the greater eternal consciousness, in my view. The Divine or Supreme consciousness is a much higher and eternal order of consciousness than man, in my view as well. Man is above nature and can fashion inanimate non-organic objects from nature, but man does not have the consciousness needed to create man from the elements. There is yet another agent of higher consciousness that is not within man's grasp. Reason tells us this is true. How? Because man exists. Man himself is evidence that the level of consciousness necessary to create man exists. That omniscient, omnipotent consciousness, exists and man himself is the evidence. In other words, it can be done, there is a way, and we are all evidence of that.

According to a Smithsonianmag.com article on the number of cells in the human body, there are about 37.2 trillion cells in the average human body.[95] Many scientists say there are 50-100 trillion. It varies according to size and height of the person. Moreover, the cells are another world or universe within themselves. Each of those trillions of cells in your body, "...has 3.4 billion letters of DNA code." That is from the BBC documentary on the cell called "The Hidden Kingdom." The BBC documentary continues, "to put it on paper has taken a hundred and twenty volumes." That is, 120 volumes of pages to describe the cell content in each one of those trillions of cells in your body! Think about that? But there is even more. The chemical elements of all DNA are essentially the same in all animals. From that DNA comes the genetic instructions to make the trillions of different cells to form your heart tissue, eye tissue, nerve tissue, bone tissue, etc. All are somehow produced from the same base chemical elements of the DNA. The DNA contains the genetic program code to make your heart and its cells, a different program code for your eyes and its unique cells, a different program code for your ears and their cells, a different program code for your fingers, toes, nose, face design, and on and on it continues. Then, there are all the other people and their genetic programming, and no two are alike. Each is a unique one of a kind. YOU are special.

A consciousness of mind with the intelligence to write a biological, genetic program code capable of arranging all 37.2 - 100 trillion cells X (46 DNA molecules per cell with 3.4 billion letters of genetic coding inside them) into the exact order to make you.

Contemplate your body and consider the level of consciousness it would take to create you, a living breathing human that has consciousness, a conscience and can think. A consciousness of mind with the intelligence to write a biological, genetic program code capable of arranging all 37.2 - 100 trillion

The single cell is like a biological computer only it is more complex than the most sophisticated computer invented by man, and it is microscopic!

cells X (46 DNA molecules per cell with 3.4 billion letters of genetic coding inside them) into the exact order to make you. Each of those cells contains 46 DNA molecules which contain 3.4 billion letters of genetic code. That amounts to about two tablespoons of DNA in your body. That is enough DNA in your body to reach the moon and back several hundred thousand times. The single cell is like a biological computer only it is more complex than the most sophisticated computer invented by man, and it is microscopic! All of this DNA life matter contains the program codes to make YOU. Now that's a programming code. We have not even begun to consider who or what wrote all this genetic coding. Moreover, who or what wrote the biological coding for all the other creatures on the earth and all of the plant life as well? Not to mention where human conscious and conscience come from. This aspect of man, so far at least, is nowhere to be found in the DNA. So where does the ghost in the machine come from? I think from the same source as love which is the kinsman to peace, which is the brother to joy, and the sister to kindness, which is the cousin to gentleness. How did these aspects of man come to be? Do you know that the arms of science cannot even begin to put its reach around these great things?

Science, too, has its limitations and we should consider this when formulating our world views. Why do we all possess the emotions of joy, peace, love, etc.? How do we all intuitively know these things are better than the opposite of them? How do we know that? Why do we prefer good even though we do not always do good? We prefer good because the source of our existence prefers it and that source prefers that we do too. Whether you believe me or not I ask you to seek your own life's journey in these matters. Do not cheat yourself by foregoing your spiritual yearnings and merely concerning yourself with only the material comforts and gadgets. They are surely fun and enjoyable to a certain degree, but only to a degree. I assure you there is a greater joy than these. If you seek it honestly, you will find it. It is written, and I believe it to be so. It is for this realm of existence, I think, that we are here. But that is my opinion, and you are under no obligation to agree. However, I think it is vital to the functioning of the machine called man yet mankind cannot even fathom its source. All the complexity of the cell that we have been looking at is only related to the physical aspects of the human body. As you keep that in mind, please consider the following quotes:

"Human DNA is like a computer program but far, far more advanced than any software we've ever created," said Bill Gates.[96]

The following is from the movie *Expelled* by Ben Stein:

Question:

Ben Stein, "If he (Darwin) thought of the cell as being a Buick, what is a cell now regarding its complexity?"

Answer:

Dr. David Berlinski: "A galaxy." (Ph.D. in Philosophy, Postdoctoral fellow in mathematics and molecular biology at Columbia University).

Question:

Ben Stein: In 1859 Darwin wrote the *Origin of the Species* and in that time "he had an idea of the cell as being quite simple, correct?"

Answer:

Dr. David Berlinski: "Yeah, everybody did."

Question:

Ben Stein, "What do we now know the cell is. What would you compare it to?"

Answer:

Dr. Michael Behe: "It's a nano-factory." (Biochemist at Lehigh University).

Question:

Ben Stein, "If Darwin thought a cell was, say, a mud hut, what do we now know that a cell is?"

Answer:

Dr. Richard Steinberg: "More complicated than a Saturn V (rocket)" (Ph.D. Systems Science / Ph.D. Biology).

Now let's consider a quote from Charles Darwin himself: "If it could be demonstrated that any complex organ existed which could not possibly have been formed by numerous, successive, slight modifications my theory would absolutely breakdown."[97]

Dr. Michael Behe of Lehigh University has developed the theory of Irreducible Complexity.[98] The theory holds that when a system is reduced to its minimally functional parts all remaining parts are each equally vital and simultaneously necessary for the particular system to function. There are parts in the cell that are interdependent and simultaneously necessary for some particular cellular functions to occur.

> *"If it could be demonstrated that any complex organ existed which could not possibly have been formed by numerous, successive, slight modifications my theory would absolutely breakdown."*
> *- Charles Darwin*

Think of it this way. A human body can live without an arm or leg for example. It can also live without eyes or ears, etc. But, what are the parts that must be simultaneously existing for a human to live? What are the bare minimum parts needed for the human body to be alive? To be specific, what is the irreducible complexity of the human body? To be alive, there must be blood, heart, brain, lungs, liver, gastro intestinal system, and pancreas. If you remove the heart, for example, the system cannot exist. If you remove the lungs, the system cannot exist. Moreover, the heart and lungs must be present simultaneously, correct? The same is true for several other parts of the human body.

Darwinian evolution argues that complexities of life systems get added or evolve along the way from the simple to the complex. However, Dr. Behe's theory of Irreducible Complexity, as I understand it, proposes that Darwin's theory of the origin of the species cannot account for the simultaneous necessity of parts for certain systems to exist. In fact, rather than the simple to the complex, I think it can be said that the exact opposite is the case. Man is a creature that appears simpler in its whole form than in his microscopic form. Life comes from the complex to the simpler. To continue with my earlier analogy, the heart and lungs would have had to evolve simultaneously for the human to exist. Behe's theory is an example of what Darwin spoke of when Darwin himself said: "If it could be demonstrated that any complex organ existed which could not possibly have been formed by numerous, successive, slight modifications my theory would absolutely breakdown."

We must remember, in fairness to Darwin and in recognition to his honesty about his own theory's weakness, that in his day the single cell was thought to be a simple blob of some sort of protoplasm. A tiny blob of life source jello. In 1859 when Darwin penned his *Origin of the Species* it was thought by many in the scientific community, that the smaller science reached into the study of life, the simpler the biological mechanisms of life would be. This thought or opinion was held by many people in this time period. Moreover, Darwin himself honestly stated that if the truth were found to be the contrary, his theory would collapse upon that reality. It couldn't be more clear that science has introduced mankind to the microscopic universe that is the single cell.

Or could it? Even with all that we now know via the progress of science over the past years since Darwin wrote his famous book there are those who still hold the view from 159 years ago. The view held by those in 1859 when it was thought the single cell was a simple organism. Consider the following from Michael Ruse and Richard Dawkins during an interview by Ben Stein in Stein's movie *Expelled.* When asked about life's origin Ruse, Philosopher of Science at Florida State University, said it, "...might have started off on the backs of crystals. Molecules piggybacked on the back of crystals forming and that this led to more and more complex, but of course the nice thing about crystals is now and then you get mistakes, mutations and that this opens the way for natural selection."[99]

Richard Dawkins, English ethologist, evolutionary biologist, and author said, "…Nobody knows how it (life) started…it could come about in the following way…a civilization evolved…and designed a form of life that they seeded on to perhaps this planet."[100]

In a short video clip from the documentary *Cosmic Origins from Big Bang to Human Kind* which Stein shows in his movie, the narrator states, "Perhaps the energy came from lightning…whatever it was...energy managed to arrange these chemical ingredients in just the right way."[101]

You will recall the quote from Bill Gates, of Microsoft Corp., that "Human DNA is like a computer program but far, far more advanced than any software we've ever created."[102] I completely agree with what Bill Gates says regarding this. Moreover, I think it is a very reasoned and rational view. For example, if I approached you or Mr. Gates with the hypothesis that his software programs were random self-ordering binary coding and he is simply the lucky person who got hold of them first, what would you think of my hypothesis? That there is no design or brains behind the programs and he just got lucky? What do you think his response would be? What is your response? Then I continue to explain my hypothesis that his subsequent programs resulting from the original were simply accidental mutations or errors that accidentally occurred along the way of writing the computer programs. Would you buy a ticket to that show? Do you believe that to be rational? Did crystals or a lucky lightning strike create Microsoft or was it conscious purpose and a well-executed plan?

Imagine your favorite animal or perhaps your pet walking in the woods, and it comes across a manmade bottle. Your pet may notice the bottle or it may not, and even though the animal is animated or alive, it is different than man in that it does not have the conscious and cognitive ability to make the bottle. This does not mean that the consciousness required to make the bottle does not exist, simply because the animal is not capable of it. The consciousness to make the bottle surely exist because the bottle exists. The needed consciousness is simply not within the ability of the animal. Enter man. Man has consciousness, is self-aware, and can think. The lower animals do not have consciousness, even though the chemical elements of DNA are similar to that of man. Pause and ponder for a moment the why of that? Man, thus, has the ability to accomplish the impossible, a miracle, from the standpoint of the lower animals.

Enter Supreme Consciousness. Man's existence, in my view, is much the same in his relationship to the Divine or Eternal Consciousness as the lower animals are to the things that man creates with his conscious ability. The lower animals, while animate, cannot conceive of the types of creations of man, much less any ability to make them themselves. In much the same way man finds himself in a world, he cannot fully conceive or comprehend. Man has his limitations just as nature and the lower animals have theirs. A bird makes its nest, but it cannot make a bottle. Man makes a bottle, but he cannot make a man. These limitations of control over the universe are where the great philosophical divide begins. At this point, some men accept they live in a world which is beyond their ability to comprehend fully, much less be in full control of. While other men refuse to accept this position and pursue a path of Darwinian evolution, humanism, materialism or physicalism, the notion that the physical universe is the only ultimate reality and there is no God, etc. In this view, life and matter are random and without purpose. Man is alone in the universe and must master it or be mastered by it. The evidence, I think, shows the latter view to be, in fact, irrational.

To this point there has only been the discussion of the things that nature forms or makes, the things that man makes, and the things that neither can make. There has been little or no mention of the origin of the raw materials to make these objects with. No mention of the origin of the laws of nature or the universe that act as the invisible design structure to the matter to make an object. The laws that govern matter, in other words. Where did the matter come from? Where did the laws of the universe come from? A couple of questions I have pondered since my early youth are: Why is there something rather that nothing? Why is there apparent order to the universe rather than random chaos? These questions not only pertain to the material matter in the universe, but also to the non-material as well.

Specifically to the natural or nature's laws that govern the universe. One could think of these laws as a kind of immutable government or body of laws of physics, mathematics, and all manner and type of science. There are also laws pertaining to the non-physical aspect of man's reality as well. These include such real human experiences such as love, hate, good, evil, happiness, and sadness, etc. In these areas however, man often believes he finds more flexibility to break the rules without apparent consequence. I am not saying there is no consequence. I am saying there is not always an apparent or immediate consequence. For this reason, man seems to, at times, act as if he were free of any immutable natural laws of behavior what so ever. In the physical world of man, if an engineering project is ill-conceived due to inaccurate application of the laws of science, there are often immediate and deadly consequences. Man learns quickly, by failing to obey the laws of nature in physics, mathematics, etc. to not make the same mistake twice. Examples are poorly engineered building structures or foundations, poorly designed or design flaws in an aircraft. You get the picture. But when man hates another there is not always the immediacy of consequence to either party to prove the particular law of moral behavior that has been breached. The consequence is hard to ascribe to a particular moral behavioral law. My only point here is to express the notion of the very real existence of the natural moral law governing the behavior of man, as well as the laws governing the physical universe. Moreover, is it not a curiosity that all men have some innate conscience of the natural moral law?

We all know, for example, the difference between an act of kindness and an act of meanness. Additionally, is it not curious that the natural moral law is the only immutable law that one could argue is innate to humanity. The laws of science, for example, are not innate to mankind. Man must seek to find or discover all of the other laws of the universe. Only the natural moral law is innate to the conscious mind of man. Mathematic laws are certainly not innate, and physics laws are not innate either, etc. Curious, is it not? I think the why of this matter is worthy of reflection and consideration. It is a truly profound reality of the human experience, and without a general and common moral understanding between all men, our existence would genuinely be a universal moral tower of Babel. We would have no hope of any just form of law to organize man's society by. This point also, I think, is worthy of reflection and consideration.

The people "...who do not have the law, do instinctively the things of the law, these, not having the law, are a law to themselves, in that they show the work of the law written in their hearts, their conscious bearing witness and their thoughts alternately accusing or else defending them" (Romans 2:14-15, New American Standard / *Founders Bible* by Shiloh Road Publisher).

So here we are. Mankind finds himself, metaphorically speaking, in a giant cosmic sandbox. In this cosmic sandbox man finds he has life, procreation ability, food and water, matter or raw material of great variety to make things with, sources of fuel, an innate moral code of behavior which gives man, at minimum, a general understanding of right and wrong behavior to organize himself among others, not innate but discoverable natural laws of science that govern the material world around him, sunlight by day, and moonlight by night, and beautiful stars in the sky to enjoy at night as well. The cosmic sandbox even has a source for money for man to use. That source is gold and silver which man has used for money for thousands of years. Big deal? Well, since you asked—Yes, it is because that gold and silver come from supernovas. Supernovas are an event that occurs when a massive star dies. When the star is dying it causes a catastrophic explosion called a Supernova. From this, we get heavy metals like gold and silver that ended up in man's cosmic sandbox.

Since the time of the ancients to modern times, mankind continues to investigate the material in his sandbox. Endlessly discovering the things that he can make with it. With the use of the raw materials and the laws of science that govern the material, man makes things like automobiles, cell phones, sailing and motor ships, computers, robotics, aircraft, spacecraft, and on and on. Man is just one piece or part of many parts in the giant cosmic sandbox. But man is a very special piece of the cosmic sandbox. Why? Because man is the only piece in the sandbox with consciousness. A mind that can think and reason. Man in his cosmic sandbox comes complete with the necessary natural laws, raw material, and a mind to create or to work with. Moreover, each one of us has natural abilities that we did not place within ourselves. Even our names were not given to ourselves by ourselves, but by our parents. In other words, none of us has placed ourselves here much less given ourselves what we have. Man has been handed everything by something other than himself. Our lives are a gift of nature and nature's God.

Man's cosmic sandbox which contains the matter and the laws of matter or science are the same now as they were thousands of years ago. The theoretical ability and scientific possibility to create the space shuttle, the cell phone, the light bulb, the computer, and on and one have always existed. Thus, in theory, none of them are new. Nothing is new under the sun. Man just thinks they are new. Man thinks he did it. Man marvels at what he does and declares certain persons that invent such fine things to be genius. A true genius would realize the fraud in such a label. To admire the invention is wonderful, admirable, and a man is due the fruits of his labor. This to be sure and never denied. But to claim the whole of the possibility seems to be a fraud. To claim the whole of the invention, a man must first create the matter out of nothing, establish the laws to govern the matter also out of nothing, then conceive of and create a truly new invention that has never before been possible in the theoretical nor the real world. Until such time humility is the more appropriate and proper response when man discovers a new, to him, this or that thing from Nature's God-given, cosmic sandbox. Man is ever advancing in his

Man is ever advancing in his understanding of his universe—but only toward what has always existed.

understanding of his universe—but only toward what has always existed. That is worthy of a full day's ponderance under a tree.

"Man cannot make, or invent, or contrive principles; he can only discover them, and he ought to look to through the discovery to the Author. When we examine an ordinary piece of machinery, an astonishing pile of architecture, a well-executed statue, or a highly finished painting...our ideas are naturally led to think of the extensive genius and talent of the artist. When we study elements of geometry, we think of Euclid. When we speak of gravitation, we think of Newton. How, then, is it that when we study the works of God in creation, we stop short and do not think of God?" writes Thomas Paine. [103]

We have all, no doubt, heard of gravity. Gravity is a constant of the universe, and it is the same for us today as it was yesterday and will be tomorrow. The speed of light is another constant. Scientists say that these "constants" are set within a very narrowly defined range. The known universe has several of these constants, and without them, we and our universe could not exist as we know it. We humans would not exist at all. One way to think of the constants is that they are the stabilizing or foundational universe forces that keep our world on earth stable and suitable for life. Imagine if gravity changed now and then. Some periods we practically floated on the surface, and other days we could hardly move under our own weight. This "unstable" force could reasonably cause fear that we may someday be crushed by the force of our weight or even float away if gravity were to continue to change dramatically. But of all the constants of the universe, there is one in particular that has gotten the attention of scientists because it is such a precisely set constant. This special constant is called the Cosmological Constant.

Leonard Susskind, the Felix Bloch Professor of Physics at Stanford University and member of the National Academy of Sciences of the U.S., explained the cosmological constant this way: "That's the one which is really on a narrow knife edge that it is almost inconceivable. If you were to change it just a tiniest, tiniest bit, we couldn't be here."[104]

Susskind goes on to say, "This cosmological constant is a kind of, it's almost a kind of anti-gravity. It's a kind of a repulsive force that is implicit in Einstein's equation for general relativity."[105]

"This cosmological constant is tuned to 1 part in 10^120, a 120 decimal places, nobody thinks that's accidental, that is not a reasonable idea, that something is tuned to 120 decimal places just by accident."[106]

To help wrap our minds around this cosmological constant and its precise setting consider the following. In a universetoday.com article about the number of atoms in the universe, it is stated it is "estimated that there are between 10^78 (ten to the seventy-eighth power) to 10^82 atoms in the known, observable universe. In layman's terms, that works out to between ten quadrillion vigintillion and one-hundred thousand quadrillion vigintillion atoms."[107] The precision of the cosmological constant is, again, 10^120 power. That is many more times than the number of atoms that is in the entire known universe.

"An honest man, armed with all the knowledge available to us now, could only state that in some sense, the origin of life appears to be at the moment to be almost a miracle, so many are the conditions which would have had to have been satisfied to get it going."
- Francis Crick

The idea that this precise setting is a matter of luck is not a rational idea. Here are the odds that the cosmological constant exists by luck. That there is one chance in 10^120 power means that there is one chance in a trillion, trillion, trillion, trillion, trillion, trillion, trillion, trillion, trillion, trillion, that the universe would be suitable for us to exist. It seems, to me, more plausible, rational, reasonable, and intellectually honest that there is order and design and purpose in this place. To my mind the chance is so great that there is no chance that this setting happened by chance. What do you think?

Scientist Francis Crick, one of the discoverers of the genetic code and an agnostic, stated "an honest man, armed with all the knowledge available to us now, could only state that in some sense, the origin of life appears to be at the moment to be almost a miracle, so many are the conditions which would have had to have been satisfied to get it going."[108]

> The movements of the heavenly bodies, so exactly held in their course by the balance of centrifugal and centripetal forces; the structure of our earth itself with its distribution of lands, waters, and atmosphere; animal and vegetable bodies examined in all their minutest particles; insects - mere atoms of life - yet as perfectly organized as man or mammoth; the mineral substances, their generation and uses; it is impossible, I say, for the human mind not to believe that there is in all this design, cause, and effect up to an Ultimate Cause - a Fabricator of all things, from matter and motion - their Preserver and Regulator while permitted to exist in their present forms - and their Regenerator into new and other forms.
>
> Thomas Jefferson[109]

Man is finite, not infinite. Man is limited in mind and body. The infinite can comprehend the finite, but the finite cannot comprehend the infinite. Man thinks in terms of beginnings and endings. That something comes from something else. That our existence is linear. That is why when a man contemplates God as eternally existing his mind goes blank, or perhaps it echoes to him that a state of eternal existence is not possible. Therefore, there is no God. Why is man limited in this way? I do not know for certain, but I have a theory that I will share in a moment. But what I do know is this; that a finite being cannot fully comprehend the infinite. Therefore, it seems to me that for the finite mind to state there is no God or Infinite Source is an elementary and grievous error of logic. The finite mind likewise cannot empirically (with direct evidence) prove that there is God either. So what is man to do? He cannot prove either case empirically. Is this a trick or some grand cosmic joke that the Infinite has played upon the finite? I do not think so at all. I think there is purpose in it. A very good and loving purpose.

I wish to propose a theory as to perhaps why we are finite and not infinite. Or at least the positive aspect of our finite nature. Suppose you and I were walking in the desert hundreds of years before glass was known, and we found a beverage bottle. Suppose neither of us has ever seen a glass beverage bottle. Both you and I, therefore, know we did not make the bottle. Also, neither of us knows how a bottle is made. The object is strange to us. But, both being the curious sort, purpose to discover the origin of the bottle. One of us proposes that a man must have made the bottle and the other proposes that that is not possible, the material is strange and unfamiliar, it must have somehow occurred naturally over time. So the quest for the truth begins, and after much searching, both of us learn exactly how bottles are made. Without the search, we would have remained in a state of ignorance concerning the bottle. But because of the search, we are now more enlightened than we previously were. It is important to note that the search was a choice that we made and we did not have to make that choice.

The bottle is a man-made object. Therefore, it is a finite object created by a finite being. The search, therefore, had a beginning and an end. Let us now take a look at our human existence and that of the universe. It is the finite searching for the infinite. Logically we know that the finite cannot know the infinite. Therefore, stop looking for *the* answer because you cannot fully, empirically know it with your finite mind. Instead start looking for answers, plural. Look at what you can know instead of what you cannot know. We know about the trillions of cells in our body and the reality of a universe that is contained in the single cell. We know that there is very advanced order in our genetic coding that makes us who we are. We know that every creature, plant, tree, fruit, etc. has its unique biological coding and that the program coding for a cat is different than a dog. The DNA genetic coding for the peach is different than the DNA of the pear, and so on. A genetic and biologic coding that is so intricate and complex that we cannot fully understand it. We know of the constants of the universe and that their precision allows us to exist. It goes on and on. We do not have the answer (and we will not until the Supreme Conscious allows) but we now have many of the answers. This information begins to add up, and we can call it evidence. This evidence tells us something of our existence. It tells us there is order to life. If there is order, it is then logical to think there is design. If there is design, then there must be purpose. It is, therefore, logical to conclude that something made you for a purpose. Some of this ordering is a natural ordering, some of it is a human ordering, and some of it is Divine or Superior Consciousness ordering. We also know that nature is not conscious and therefore does not and is not capable of conscious order or design.

> The human mind is not capable of grasping the Universe. We are like a little child entering a huge library. The walls are covered to the

> ceilings with books in many different tongues. The child knows that someone must have written these book. It does not know who or how. It does not understand the languages in which they are written. But the child notes a definite plan in the arrangement of the books - a mysterious order which it does not comprehend, but only dimly suspects.
>
> Albert Einstein[110]

Choose any man-made invention you like, the more complex, the better. A space craft, a super computer, a simple cell phone, etc. Now imagine that it is your job to convince someone that nobody made it. It just appeared. You probably find it hard even to know where to begin doing that, right? You should because it is not logical. You may not be able consciously to explain the technology, nor can I, but we both know on some sub-conscious level that it did not self-manufacture. We both know that idea or notion is less than rational. It is not rational. Your genetic makeup, the cell, for example, are both far more advanced than a super computer or a rocket yet the notion that you mindlessly evolved without purpose continues to be advanced by some.

> *Albert Einstein also states, "Everyone who is seriously involved in the pursuit of science becomes convinced that a spirit is manifest in the laws of the Universe—a spirit vastly superior to that of man, and one in the face of which we with our modest powers must feel humble."*

Albert Einstein also states, "Everyone who is seriously involved in the pursuit of science becomes convinced that a spirit is manifest in the laws of the Universe—a spirit vastly superior to that of man, and one in the face of which we with our modest powers must feel humble."[111]

For all of the above reasons and more that I cannot possibly list here, I think it is logical to conclude we are no more an accident of an unconscious state of nature than the bottle. The bottle is nothing compared to you and your Divine construction yet you would think me ridiculous if I tried to convince you it evolved and millions like it continue to evolve. Neither is an accident of nature. The bottle nor the man. Your own reasoning ability is likely telling you this is so. But just like the men in the desert, you can choose whether or not to think of it. You can choose not to search.

So what is it? Is our existence a stroke of cosmological luck that piggybacked on a crystal or is there evidence to support something more. For me, the answer is self-evident at this point. There appear to be tremendous volumes of evidence of order and design to life itself and the natural universe. A question? Do you believe in science? Where is science? Can you see science? No. So why do you believe? Why does one believe in science that he cannot see and consider it logical and reasonable? We believe in science because of the evidence of science. One cannot use science to prove science, but we can use the evidence of science to reason the probable existence of science. By the same thread of logic, we can reason the evidence of our Creator. From this point onward, in both matters of God and science in the search, it is faith. We have faith that the same laws of science that worked today will work tomorrow. If you did not, you would not likely get on your next flight. You have faith in the existence and reliability of science. It is this same reason by evidence that it is logical to have faith in God. A reasoned, rational, and logical faith. Faith from the ever-growing body of evidence and that is important.

Why? Because this discovery of evidence keeps the finite man searching. When a man discovers the answer to anything the search is over, right? You stop looking. The Supreme Consciousness or God is infinite. Therefore, man getting to know the Mind of God, so to speak, never ends. This is a good thing, not a bad one. To know the Infinite is to be on an Infinite path of discovery. The search to know God or Infinite Supreme Conscious continues, but most importantly so do the discoveries all along the way, and that is the beautiful part. This is the positive aspect of our finite existence—the journey to know God. This is why, I think, faith is the logical choice.

> "In consideration of the cosmos, the order of the universe which I with my limited human mind can perceive, yet there are those who say there is no God. What makes me angry is when they quote me in support of such views."
>
> Albert Einstein[112]

Einstein also said, "The important thing is not to stop questioning. Curiosity has its own reason for existing. One cannot help but be in awe when he contemplates the mysteries of eternity, of life, of the marvelous structure of reality. It is enough if one tries merely to comprehend a little of this mystery every day. Never lose a holy curiosity."[113] This statement sums up Einstein's deepest feelings. "I want to know how God created this world. I am not interested in this or that phenomenon, in the spectrum of this or that element. I want to know his thoughts; the rest are details."[114]

The following may seem silly at first, but there is a serious and profound point to be made. The point is supported at the end with a few quotes from notable people.

God says to the world that "I'm coming to the earth tomorrow at noon eastern time. I will be at New York's Times Square. It will be a short visit. I will leave a book for humanity. A book titled and explaining the Theory of Everything." Finally, man will get the answers he has always sought—the proof of God from God's book no less. So God does as he says and leaves the book at Times Square, N.Y.

When the Book is opened all mankind learns two things. 1. The Book contains the science of everything in the universe. All of the answers to man's questions. 2. Most all of mankind, if not all, now know no more than they did before God came back to earth. This is true because only a few men on earth can take the Book and even begin to understand it. The majority of the science seems far beyond that of our greatest scientists' ability to comprehend. This leaves the common man totally in the blind. Even the scientists declare that it will take years, if not an eternity, to even begin to decipher the Book.

Mankind now begins to grumble and gets mad at God for leaving a Book about everything that explains, in an understandable way, nothing. Man is angry, and God is even now hated by more of mankind than before.

God sees what is happening and so He calls back to earth and says, "I'll be back tomorrow at noon to explain why I left that Book." God does and says, "The last time I left you all a Book you complained it was too simple to be believed."

A famous Nobel Laureate, Bertrand Russell, who held a B.A. in Philosophy, a mathematician, and logician, when asked what he would say if he met God upon death famously replied: "I should reproach him for not giving us enough evidence."[115]

A famous scientist, Albert Einstein, who gave us the theory of relativity once said as to the possibility and result of science explaining everything. "It would be possible to describe everything scientifically, but it would make no sense; it would be without meaning as if you described a Beethoven symphony as a variation of wave pressure."[116]

Another famous Book describes it this way, "For the whole law is fulfilled in one word, in the statement, 'You shall love your neighbor as yourself'" (Galatians 5:14).

The secular man declares a theory that life began with a Big Bang, and the world applauds in awe of the genius of the theory.

The Christian Bible declares in Genesis, in the opening chapter, "In the beginning, God created the heavens and the earth. Then God said, 'Let there be light,'" and many in the world ridicule and laugh.

Now we are back where we began, and I still see no conflict or bifurcation between God and science. I would imagine that when God spoke His universe into existence, there was quite a... Big Bang!

The Takeaway for Freedom's Defense: God cannot be proved or disproved, but nature's laws are rational, have clear evidence of design, and are the self-evident foundation for the individual rights and liberty of man. That is why faith is the logical choice.

END NOTES

[1] "Feminist Conference Says Clapping Triggers Anxiety," March 24, 2015, Washingtontimes.com.

[2] "21 Racial Micro Aggressions You Hear on a Daily Basis," December 9, 2013, Buzzfeed.com.

[3] "Why I use Trigger Warnings," September 19, 2015, NYtimes.com.

[4] "Banned Books that Shaped America," bannedbooksweek.org.

[5] William Jay, "The Life of John Jay," (New York: J&J Harper,1833), vol.1 p.82 "John Jay's Charge to the Grand Jury During the First Term of the New York State Supreme Court," Wallbuilders.com.

[6] James Madison, The Writings of James Madison, Gaillard Hunt, editor (New York: G.P. Putnam's Sons, 1906), Vol.VI p.102, "Property," Originally published in "The National Gazette" on March 29, 1792, Wallbuilders.com

[7] *The Writings of Thomas Jefferson*, H.A. Washington, editor (New York: Riker, Thorne, & Co.,1854), Vol. VIII P 147, to the society of the Methodist Episcopal Church at New London, CT, on February 4,1809, Wallbuilders.com/biblical-Christianity-origin-rights-Conscience/#FN34 Thomas Jefferson

[8] "The History of Poisoned Alcohol Included an Unlikely Culprit: The U.S. Government," January 14, 2015, Time.com

[9] *The Communist Manifesto,* Karl Marx & Frederick Engels, International Publishers Co., Inc. 1948. This printing 2015. 24.

[10] Ibid. 25.

[11] "We Need to Punish Climate Change Deniers and Put a Price on Carbon," March 16, 2016, Ecowatch.com.

[12] "Robert Kennedy Jr. Wants to Jail His Political Opponents - Accuses Koch Brothers of Treason - They Ought to be Serving Time for It," September 12, 2014, Climatedepot.com.

[13] John Leland. *The Sacred Rights of Conscience*, Liberty Fund, Publishers, Inc. 2009, page 340, Edited by Daniel Dreisbach and Mark David Hall.

[14] Ibid, 339.

[15] John Locke, *Two Treatise of Government*, Chapter II sec. 4.

[16] *Founder's Bible*, Shiloh Road Publishers LLC, 2012, Articles written by historian David Barton, 277.

[17] John Locke, *Two Treatise of Government,* Chapter XVIII Of Tyranny sec. 199.

[18] https://www.azquotes.com/quote/867275, accessed December 25, 2017.

[19] Mark Levin, *Liberty and Tyranny*, Threshold Editions, A Division of Simon and Shuster, Inc., 29.

[20] Alexis de Tocqueville, *Democracy in America*, Bantam Classics, copyright 2000, 13.

[21] Sam Adams, Essay In The Public Advertiser, 1749, https://foundersquotes.com.

[22] Thomas Paine, *The American Crisis*, "The Crisis IV," Philadelphia, April 19. 1777, Collected and Edited by Moncure Daniel Conway. 1774-1779.

[23] "Andrew Jackson Farewell Address, The American Presidency Project, March 4, 1837, www.ucab.edu/ws/index.php?pid+67087.

[24] Thomas Paine, *The American Crisis*, "The Crisis," Philadelphia, April 19. 1777, Collected and Edited by Moncure Daniel Conway. 1774-1779.

[25] "IRS Should Return its Ill-gotten Gain," February 17, 2016, USA.com.

[26] "Maryland Dairy Farmer Beats The IRS - Will Recover Nearly $30,000 Seized Through Forfeiture," June 26, 2016, www.Forbes.com.

[27] "Sweet Cakes by Melissa, Christian Bakers from Oregon, Appeal $135K Fine in Gay Wedding Case." March 26, 2017, Washingtontimes.com

[28] Eddie Stannard, "Fabian Socialist George Bernard Shaw in His Own words," www.youtube.com/watch?v=t31BdyFrPps.

[29] "The Papers of Benjamin Franklin," Packard Humanities Institute. http://franklinpapers.org/franklin/framedVolumes.jsp?vol=6&page=238a, 87.

[30] James Madison quote, Constitution Society, Federalist 39, www.constitution.org/fed/federal39.htm, www.themoneymasters.com/the-money-masters/famous-quotations-on-banking/

[31] Thomas Paine, www.thomaspaine.us/article_bisheff01.html

[32] "De Blazio Dropping Plans for Uber Cap for Now" July 23, 2015, NYTimes.com

[33] "Congress Still on Track to be among Least Productive in Recent History," September 23, 2014, pewresearch.org.

[34] "Red Tapeworm 2014: A Record Number of Federal Register Final Rule Pages," June 25, 2014, cei.org/blog/red-tapeworm.

[35] July 23, 2015, usdebtclock.org, Congressional Budget Office.

[36] "Pathogens Causing Us Foodborne Illnesses, Hospitalizations, and Deaths, 2000-2008," July 23, 2015, CDC.gov.

[37] FAERS (Federal Adverse Event Reporting System) reporting by patient outcomes by year, FDA.gov.

[38] "Chicago murder rate," nymag.com/daily/intelligencer/2016/03/Chicago-murder-rate-is-way-up-this-year.html

[39] "Chicago murder rate," nymag.com/daily/intelligencer/2016/03/Chicago-murder-rate-is-way-up-this-year.html

[40] "The Inexplicable War on Lemonade Stands," Eric Kain, June 28, 2016, http://forbes.com/sites/erikkain/2011/08/03/the-inexplicable-war-on-lemonade-stands.

[41] "Democracy in America," Alexis de Tocqueville 1835, Bantam Classics, 2000, 862.

[42] Thomas Jefferson, First Inaugural, March 4, 1801, https://wallbuilders.com/analyzing-legistation.

[43] Baron de Montesquieu, *The Spirit of the Laws*, New York, D. Appleton & Company, https://books.google.com/books?=NMdEAQAAMAAJ, Vol. I 258.

[44] Josiah Stamp, Wind and Fly LTD, 2017, http://www.AZquotes.com/quote/679677, accessed December 28, 2017, AZquotes.com.

[45] James Madison,www.themoneymasters.com/the-money-masters/famous-quotations-on-banking/

[46] Thomas Jefferson, www.themoneymasters.com/the-money-masters/famous-quotations-on-banking/

[47] Bonnie Alba, “Debt Dishonors and Destroys our Nation,” November 19, 2010, www.renewamerica.com/columns/Alba/101119.

[48] Henry Ford, www.themoneymasters.com/the-money-masters/famous-quotations-on-banking/

[49] Sir Josiah Stamp, Director Bank of England, www.themoneymasters.com/the-money-masters/famous-quotations-on-banking/

[50] George Bancroft, *History of the United States*, Little Brown, and Company, 1854, vol. I, 315.

[51] George Percy, “’A Trewe Relacyon’ Virginia from 1609-1612,” Tyler’s Quarterly Historical and Genealogical Magazine, ed. Lyon G. Tyler, Richmond VA, Richmond Press, Inc. 1922, Vol. 3, No. 1, 266-267

[52] William Bradford, *Of Plymouth Plantation,* ed. Samuel Eliot Morison, New York: Alfred A. Knopf, 1991, 120-121.

[53] Ibid.

[54] Richard J. Maybury, “The Great Thanksgiving Hoax,” Nov. 27 2014, mises.org.

[55] *Humanist Manifestos I and II,* Prometheus Books, 1973 Edited by Paul Kurtz.

[56] ww.americanthinker.com/articles/…/Never_Call_Socialism _By_Its_Right_Name.html.

[57] Karl Marx & Frederich Engels, *The Communist Manifesto,* International Publishers NY, 1948, current copy, 2015.

[58] President Johnson's Great Society Speech, www.presidency.ussb.edu/ws/?pid=26262

[59] Ibid.

[60] Ibid.

[61] Ibid.

[62] Paul Harvey, "From Freedom to Chains," radio address, https://www.youtube.com/watch?v=n0FF13u13WE

[63] "Pocket Constitution," Cato Institute, 2004.

[64] Thomas Jefferson quote, Letter to Francois Divernois, February 6, 1795, https://founders.archives.gov/documents/Jefferson/01-28-02-0196.

[65] "A Response to Cato's Fourth Through Seventh Letters..." www.thomas-paine-friends.org/paine-thomas_a-responde-to-cato-1776-03.htm

[66] William Bradford, *Of Plymouth Plantation,* Published by The Vision Forum, Inc. and Mantle Ministries, 2004, 8.

[67] www.bbc.co.uk/history/people/william_tyndale/

[68] George Bancroft, *The History of the United States,* Little, Brown, and Company, vol. I. 299.

[69] Mr. Cooper, *The History of North America,* W.S. Marsh, 1814, 36.

[70] George Bancroft, *The History of the United States,* Little, Brown, and Company, vol. I. 299.

[71] *Founder's Bible*, Shiloh Road Publishers LLC, 2012, Articles written by historian David Barton.

[72] www.ushistory.org/Paine/commonsense/sense1.htm.

[73] Joel Dorman Steele, Ph.D., F.G.S. and Esther Baker Steele, Lit, D., *Barnes Historical Series - A Brief History of the United States*, American Book Company, by 102.

[74] Ibid. 103-104.

[75] Ibid. 102-103.

[76] Ibid. 103-104.

[77] Ibid. 104-105.

[78] Ibid. 105.

[79] Thomas Paine, "The American Crisis," Philadelphia, Jan. 13, 1777.

[80] Joel Dorman Steele, Ph.D., F.G.S. and Esther Baker Steele, Lit, D., *Barnes Historical Series / A Brief History of the United States*, American Book Company, 113.

[81] "Tea Parties—Same Song, Second Verse, wallbuilders.com/tea-parties-song-second-verse/#FN13.

[82] Mr. Cooper, *The History of North America,* W.S. Marsh, 1814.

[83] Ibid. 264.

[84] Ibid.

[85] Ibid.

[86] Ibid.

[87] Ibid.

[88] Ibid.

[89] Ibid.

[90] Ibid.

[91] liberty-virtue-independence-blogspot.com.

[92] *The Life of John Jay,* vol. 1 519-520, Wallbuilders.com

[93] https://wallbuilders.com/in-god-we-trust/

[94] *Humanist Manifestos I and II,* Prometheus Books, 1973 Edited by Paul Kurtz.

[95] Rose Eveleth, "There are 37.2 Trillion Cells in your Body," October 24, 2013, Smithsonianmag.com.

[96] https://evolutionnews.org/2017/07/we-hold-these-truths-to-be-self-evident/ "We Hold These Truths to be Self-Evident," Evolutions News, December 6, 2017.

[97] Darwin-online.org.uk/Variorum/1860-189-c-1859.html.

[98] www.ideacenter.org/contentmgr/showdetails.php/id/840.

[99] http://www.youtube.com/watch?v=AOPkXFTd5RS

[100] https://www.youtube.com/watch?v=GIZtEjtlirc.

[101] http://www.youtube.com/watch?v=AOPkXFTd5RS

[102] https://evolutionnews.org/2017/07/we-hold-these-truths-to-be-self-evident/ "We Hold These Truths to be Self-Evident," Evolutions News, December 6, 2017.

[103] *Founder's Bible*, Shiloh Road Publishers LLC, 2012, Articles written by historian David Barton,4.

[104] https://www.youtube.com/watch?v=2cT4zZIHR3s&t=248s.

[105] Ibid.

[106] https://www.youtube.com/watch?v=nXi_YADO9ZI&t=79s.

[107] http://www.universetoday.com/36302/atoms-in-the-universe/

[108] https://quotefancy.com/quote/1149784/Francis-Crick-An-honest-man-armed-with-all-the-knowledge-available-to-us-now-could-only

[109] *Founder's Bible*, Shiloh Road Publishers LLC, 2012, Articles written by historian David Barton, 5.

[110] http://www.simpletoremember.com/articles/a/Einstein/

[111] Ibid.

[112] Blogs.christianpost.com/nutshell/god-particle-proof-of-god-in-the-smallest-parts-10711/

[113] http://www.simpletoremember.com/articles/a/Einstein/

[114] Ibid.

[115] www.saintsandskeptics.org/the-evidence-for-god/

[116] http://thinkexist.com/quotation/it_would_be_possible_to_describe_everything/15520.html, Albert Einstein quotes - ThinkExist.com.

Made in the USA
Columbia, SC
07 July 2018